To Deborah,
May your path
be filled with learning
power. Best wishes,

Dm Tafladr

POWERLEARNING

DONALD J. LOFLAND, Ph.D.

*P*OWERLEARNING

MEMORY

AND

LEARNING

TECHNIQUES

FOR

PERSONAL

POWER

LONGMEADOW PRESS

Excerpts from *The Techniques of Reading*, Third Edition, by Horace Judson, © 1972 by The Reading Laboratory Inc. Reprinted with permission by Harcourt Brace Jovanovich, Inc.

Powerlearning is a registered trademark of Powerlearning® Systems, P.O. Box 496, Santa Cruz, CA 95060

Illustrations by Melani Gendron-Lofland and Donald Lofland
Cover design by Frank Stinga
Interior design by Fritz Metsch

LIBRARY OF CONGRESS CATALOGING-IN-PUBLICATION DATA
Lofland, Donald J.
   Powerlearning : states for learning, memory, personal power :
innovative learning methods to gain your personal power / by Donald
J. Lofland.
     p. cm.
  Includes index.
  ISBN: 0-681-41574-6
   1. Success—Psychological aspects. 2. Neurolinguistic
programming. 3. Learning, Psychology of. 4. Mnemonics. 1. Title.
BF637.S8L574 1992
153.1—dc20   92-9733
                                           CIP

PRINTED IN THE UNITED STATES OF AMERICA

First Edition

0 9 8 7 6 5 4 3 2 1

DEDICATION

This work is dedicated to Clyde A. Lofland,
my dad, who introduced me to physics, a
curiosity for how things work, and a role
model of how to live life with fullness . . .

&

in memory of Dana Butterfield,
who knew the secret,
of living wholly,
here and now,
one's uniqueness.

ACKNOWLEDGMENTS

I'd like to express my gratitude to the many people who have helped make this work possible . . .

- Frank Weimann, my agent, who never lost faith in Powerlearning;
- My dedicated editors Diane Frank and Pamela Altschul;
- Melanie Gendron-Lofland, my illustrator
- Dr. Donald Schuster who introduced this country and me personally to accelerated learning methods;
- Doris Richardson, whose unwavering faith in my work and help with mechanical details got me through the final days of completion.

CONTENTS

PART ONE

POWERLEARNING AND STATES

CHAPTER ONE

LEARNING: TO GET WHAT YOU WANT IN LIFE

Educational therapists are beginning to realize that almost anyone can potentially learn anything . . . it's just a matter of establishing a *learning state* that works for each person. This book or any other cannot actually teach you *how* to learn. You are a superb learner already. Just getting up this morning, doing your daily activities, moving your body, etc., you have automatically learned thousands of impressions and bits of information. Having the motivation to read this book means you probably already have what it will take to succeed.

The secret is in how to set up states—for learning, memory, and personal power. Then it is easy to get the results we want and deserve.

What, then, is learning? When we think about learning, we usually think of a classroom or training seminar. Learning is actually much broader than that. Do you encounter new learning in any of the following?

- hobbies
- relationships
- staying healthy
- getting ahead in your career
- sports and recreation

Learning is probably the fabric of being alive. Consider, then, some of the *advantages* of improving your learning skills:[1]

- clearer thinking
- more money and a better job
- improvement with hobbies
- improved relationships
- better health
- higher self-esteem
- learning more in less time
- having fun learning new things

Consider the disadvantages of not improving your learning skills:

- foggy thinking
- less knowledge
- frustrating relationships
- poor self-esteem
- making less money
- fewer hobbies
- worse health
- shorter life

Finally, consider the "benefits" of not improving your learning skills; You:

- keep psychiatrists and counselors in business
- leave high-paying jobs for others
- don't have to risk the possibility of failure
- avoid the demands of increased responsibility
- won't threaten others by appearing brilliant

THOSE SPECIAL DAYS

Men stumble over truth from time to time, but most pick themselves up and continue off as if nothing had happened.

—*Sir Winston Churchill*

One great truth is that all days are not created equal. Why is it that every once in a while we have one of those special days where everything seems to go our way? We do just the right thing at the right time . . . the tennis game is exceptional . . . or we come up with all the right answers in an important meeting. Sometimes it seems that we couldn't have planned the day better. Of course, another question might be, "Why don't we have special days more often?"

```
--------------------------------------------------------------
|                                                            |
|                        EXERCISE 1                          |
|                        ──────────                          |
|                                                            |
|    Take a piece of paper and list all the qualities you    |
| can think of that make those special days unique. How do   |
| you feel physically? What emotions do you feel? How does   |
| the world look? Do you notice any special sounds? Take a   |
| minute or two and write down as many characteristics as    |
| quickly as you can.                                        |
|                                                            |
| Here are some of the most frequently listed qualities.     |
| Check them against your list:                              |
|                                                            |
|    • I feel relaxed.                                       |
|    • Everything falls into place.                          |
|    • I feel spontaneous.                                   |
|    • I am happy and energetic.                             |
|    • The day looks brighter.                               |
|    • Things really click for me.                           |
|    • Other people pick up on my mood.                      |
|    • These days are too rare!                              |
|                                                            |
| How do these qualities compare with your experience?       |
|                                                            |
--------------------------------------------------------------
```

What sets these days apart is the neurological *state* we are in. Psychologists might say we are in an empowering state or a resourceful state. This state of being allows us to feel inner strength, confidence, joy, or peak performance. At other times we may experience paralyzing states that leave us fearful, depressed, confused, and unable to act. Our performance in life and our ability to learn are direct results of the state we are in.

Would you be interested in having those special days more often? We will discuss two powerful keys to create states for getting the results we want, in both learning and daily living.

WHAT ARE STATES?

Pat could hardly wait for her first date with John, the new marketing director. She was in a *state* of anticipation. When she arrived and *saw* the flowers he had brought, she experienced a *state* of gratitude. When she *heard* him compliment her dress, she experienced another state, and when she *felt* indigestion from his cooking, she experienced yet another state. A state is the sum of millions of neurological processes happening within us at any point in time. The states we experience may be empowering or limiting, but mostly they are unconscious reactions to what we see, hear, feel, smell, or taste. We need to learn to choose the states we desire.

Each state we experience results in the brain producing certain chemical substances—neuropeptides and neurotransmitters. As an example, when we feel powerful and invincible, our brains produce a substance similar to interleukin 2, one of the most powerful substances known to destroy cancer cells. When we feel calm and settled, we produce a natural tranquilizer similar to Valium. When the brain produces these substances, we experience none of the undesirable side effects we would if we had injected or ingested these or similar drugs. The brain and body in their inherent wisdom know just how much of each substance to produce and how and where to distribute them.

A fascinating characteristic of states is that not only the brain experiences the state, but also the whole body experiences it. Each cell in the body has neuroreceptors for receiving the chemical "signals" (neuropeptides and neurotransmitters) put out by the brain. Thus, as Dr. Deepak Chopra points out in *Quantum Healing*, when people feel jittery, the brain produces high levels of epinephrine and norepinephrine. However, blood platelets also have neuroreceptors for these substances, so the platelets as well as the brain experience the jitteriness. When we are sad, neuroreceptors in the kidneys, stomach, and skin pick up the transmitters corresponding to sadness, so our kidneys, stomach, and skin are also sad. When we are happy, our whole body is exposed to substances that fight viruses and bacteria. We wind up with happy eyes and a happy heart.

There is further evidence that other cells outside the brain produce the same neuropeptides and neurotransmitters. Dr. Chopra postulates that each cell in the body may produce all of these substances, so in a sense each cell has its own mind to produce and experience states.

What most of us want in life—happiness, love, comfort, power, success, etc.—are simply states.

EXERCISE 2

Quickly write down five of your most important goals in life. Next to each write why you would like to achieve that goal.

Is one of your goals related to having more money? If so, why do you want more money? You might respond that you could buy certain things. I would ask further why you want to buy those things. Perhaps you would reply that it makes you feel powerful to be able to buy what you want. *Feeling powerful*, then, is the state you are after, and having money is one means to achieve that state. If your goal is to be in a relationship, again, that is not likely the core goal. Why do you want to be in a relationship? Maybe you love the feeling of being in love, or maybe you feel more secure in a relationship, or maybe you feel more connected with a sense of companionship. Again, these states are the real goals. Having a new car might provide you with a state of freedom. Having a spiritual path might provide you with more meaning in life.

PURPOSE

CHANGING STATES

Most of us assume that states just happen to us, and they depend on external circumstances: "If only I had this job . . ."; "If only I had this home . . ."; "If only this person would marry me . . ."; "If only that person would divorce me." Goals as a means to achieve states are certainly fine, but we don't have to wait for external circumstances to change to enjoy the states we want. In fact, being in a resourceful state is a prerequisite to accelerating learning, learning is a means to achieve our goals, and achieving the goals provides states we desire.

Can we learn to change our states without having to ingest drugs or wait for the right set of external circumstances? Evidence that we have the potential to direct these seemingly involuntary states comes from research on one of the most intriguing mental disorders: multiple personality syndrome.

Researchers have studied MPS patients such as Eve, with dozens of different personalities. Each one produced states totally inconsistent with the other personalities. For example, one of Eve's personalities was allergic to bee stings—so much so that a sting could produce a life-threatening reaction. When another of her personalities kicked in, however, the reaction disappeared. One personality required glasses, while another had 20/20 vision.

Most of us change our state as an unconscious reaction to people or events around us. The first keys to direct our states *consciously* are:

1. *Physiology*. How do we feel physically? Are we rested? Are we tired? Are we energetic? Often when we have special days, it's after a good night's sleep, or a dynamic exercise session, or any situation in which we feel physically alive and vibrant.

2. *Internal representations*. How does our brain represent or model the world around us? As human beings we are totally fascinated with creating models. The hour hand on a clock models the apparent movement of the sun across the sky. Physics equations represent the way nature works. A map is a model of the layout of the land.

   Our senses also create a model. When light hits the retina of the eye, an electrochemical impulse travels to the brain. The brain doesn't directly perceive the light, but rather the electrochemical signal. The same is true of hearing. The brain doesn't directly perceive the sound, but instead the electrochemical signal generated by nerve endings within the ear. And so it is with each of the senses.

   Our conclusion has to be that we do not directly perceive reality at all, but rather a neurological *model* created by our senses. This, our internal model of the universe, together with out attitudes, belief systems, and learning strategies, constitute our *internal representations*, which I will abbreviate IR's.

Understand that our IR's do not precisely represent what is happening around or within us. Consciously, we focus on one or several things at a time, so that most perception is filtered out unconsciously. Our attitudes and belief systems can also cause distortions, generalizations, and deletions in our perceptions.

Do we see the color blue in the same way . . . or hear the same sounds at a concert? I doubt it. More likely we each have completely unique internal representations of these and other experiences. Certainly our attitudes, belief systems, and strategies for dealing with life are unique. Our IR's are probably as individual as snowflakes. Why, then, does our educational system treat us as if we all learned in the same way?

Going back to those special days, we can say that our behavior and performance are determined by our state, and our state is determined by our physiology and IR's.

STATES AND LEARNING
- -

Think of just one area (a hobby, a type of reading, a sport, or an academic subject) in which you have found it easy and fun to learn. Simply, you were "in state" for this type of learning. Suppose, on the other hand, you find math, foreign languages, relationships, or advancing your career particularly difficult. Evidently you haven't learned how to put yourself into a resourceful state for that type of learning.

You must then learn how to change your state. This requires that you change your physiology, or change your internal representations, or both.

EXERCISE 3

Following is a list of twenty terms. Look them over for thirty seconds. Then take a piece of paper and write out the twenty terms from memory, preferably in the same order. Write as many as you can. Stop reading until you have completed this.

1. book
2. key
3. camera
4. bowl
5. cereal
6. three
7. compass
8. orange
9. tree
10. bird
11. fork
12. grasshopper
13. road
14. cough drop
15. teakettle
16. cloud
17. balloon
18. New York City
19. box
20. surprise

Once you have written the twenty words from memory, go back and check out your results against the list.

EXERCISE 4

Now let's approach the previous exercise in a different way. Stand up and stretch for a couple of minutes. If it is not convenient to stand, stretch while sitting. Take a deep breath, close your eyes, and let your whole body go limp for about thirty seconds. With each breath you exhale, let your body become more relaxed.

Next, get yourself into a comfortable position and imagine a friend of yours giving you a *book*. Attached to the book is a large golden *key*. You take the key, unlock the book, and discover a *camera* inside. You pick up the camera and take a picture of a large *bowl*. You are hungry and so delighted to see the bowl filled with your favorite *cereal*. As you eat your way down to the bottom, you notice a large number *three*. After looking more closely, you notice the three is the number on a large *compass*. You see the compass needle pointing outside, toward a nice, juicy *orange*. The orange is hanging from a *tree*. Sitting on one of the branches is a *bird*, and you are quite surprised to see the bird feeding its young ones with a *fork*. As you look closer, you are disgusted to see that on the fork is a *grasshopper*, but the grasshopper jumps down onto the *road*. Suddenly rolling down the road comes a large *cough drop*, which rolls into a nearby *teakettle*. The teakettle begins to boil up into a *cloud*, which now shapes itself into a large passenger *balloon*. You decide to go for a ride, so after a while you are way up in the sky looking down on *New York City*. As you look carefully, on the ground there is a very large *box*. Suddenly from out of the box jumps a *surprise*. The surprise is a part of you who wants you to know that you have a better memory than you think! Now take another deep breath and write the twenty terms, or as many as you remember.

Why was the exercise easier the second time? Most people better their scores because they have changed their state to one in which it is easier to remember the words. We first changed our physiology with stretching, a deep breath, and relaxation. Then we changed our internal representation by putting the words into the context of a story and using *visual imagery*. If your score significantly improved, you were more in state for this type of learning.

What does it mean if your score didn't improve that much? It may simply imply that this story, which uses *visual* imagery, did not work for you. You may do much better with the auditory and kinesthetic techniques, which will be discussed later.

But what is important is that you can discover the learning strategies that will put you in a state to facilitate both learning and having more of those special days. And that is what Powerlearning® is all about.

GETTING TO KNOW YOUR INTERNAL REPRESENTATIONS

Our internal representations or IR's allow us to "make sense" of reality. Four qualities of IR's are particularly important to accelerate learning. These are:

1. *Thinking styles—visual, auditory, or kinesthetic (VAK).*

   "You aren't *listening* to what I've *told* you. I've *explained* a hundred times that you have to keep your room clean," snapped Mrs. Schmidt at her teenage son.

   "But I just don't *see* why", he replied. "It's not *clear*. You don't have to live in here, and it *looks* just fine to me."

   "Maybe we should share our *feelings* and get a *handle* on this," interjected Mr. Schmidt. You can imagine why the Schmidts aren't communicating. They think differently!

   How do *you* learn most easily? By seeing—*visual (V)*? By hearing—*auditory (A)*? Or by feeling or doing—*kinesthetic (K)*? Our unconscious takes in data from all the senses all the time, but within our IR's we generally prefer one or two modes.

   About 60 percent of all people are primarily visual learners and thinkers. They need to *see* a picture or *visualize* what is going on. When this mode is most developed, the person is said to have a *photographic memory*: "Oh, I remember the answer to that question! It was on page thirty-seven, second paragraph, third line." Visuals are usually the fastest learners. They quickly see the picture and are ready to move on.

About 25 percent of people are primarily auditory, learning and thinking through hearing. Remember back to a class you took. Do you recall that one person who would just sit there and listen, who didn't take notes, and yet got it? Auditory learners can often pick up foreign languages very quickly by simply listening. Trivia champions are often auditory.

The other 15 percent of people are primarily kinesthetic, learning by feelings, touch, and movement. A kinesthetic learner has to get a feel for how it works. A kinesthetic learner usually learns best by doing. Einstein was primarily kinesthetic. Champion athletes are also superb kinesthetic learners.

LEARNING STYLES

Even though we consciously prefer one or two of the visual, auditory, or kinesthetic modes (V, A, or K), all of us use a combination of all three. Our individual combination is unique. In a group of fifty people I doubt that any two would have exactly the same combination.

Most teachers and study guides assume that we all learn in the same way. This is most unfortunate. In Chapter Three, you will test yourself to discover your thinking and learning style. Psychologists and counselors will often do more extended testing to give you a personal profile, but they don't tell you how to change your style. We will learn techniques to change your IR's. Then, you can change your mode to V, A, or K to match the specific learning task at hand.

---

2. *Brain functioning style.* The human brain has two sides—the right side, or right cerebral hemisphere, and the left side, or left cerebral hemisphere. Each side has its own specialized way of thinking and remembering. Most people tend to function more from one side than the other. For example, accountants and technicians will often function more from the left side, while artists and dancers will function more from the right.

We actually use both halves of our brain all the time, but most of us prefer to function more from one side or the other. More and more books are talking about how the right and left sides of the brain tie in with thinking and learning. However, very few tell you how to change your IR's by shifting toward functioning more from either the right or the left side. Later you will learn some simple brain "shifters" to match your brain functioning to the task at hand—whether it is learning, improving a relationship, or dealing with your boss or a client.

3. *Magic keys.* Related to visual, auditory, and kinesthetic learning are *keys*, sometimes called *magic keys*—the order in which we take external data and process them internally. On a crucial point in a tennis match, you might see your second serve sailing long. That is external visual input. You scold yourself mentally (internal auditory) and then feel depressed (internal kinesthetic). The key is the sequence: external visual—>internal auditory—>internal kinesthetic, which leads to a state called *depression*.

We all have distinct combinations of visual, auditory, and kinesthetic experience—both external and internal—that result in a variety of states. We each have one key to convince us to buy something, another key to become motivated, and still another for falling in love. A key is the mental combination or recipe for producing a particular state.

Once we discover our own unconscious key for motivation, we can consciously use that key whenever we want to be motivated. If we learn the unconscious key all good spellers use to be successful with spelling, we can model their key to become a good speller.

Neurolinguistic programming, abbreviated *NLP*, is a branch of psychology that in part analyzes unconscious keys we as individuals use to produce various states. NLP researchers also seek to discover unconscious keys used by the most successful achievers in sports, sales, politics, and various branches of learning. They study people who have rewarding relationships, people who can get themselves highly motivated, people who can overcome allergies, people who learn effectively, and generally people who are happy and successful. The results of using NLP for personal growth and therapy are both profound and quick.

4. *Models*. These are personal heroes, actors, friends, and famous people we use as images to help mold our behavior and growth. Just decide what you want—wealth, a relationship, better memory, technical knowledge, or a better tennis game. Find someone who produces the results you want. If you can learn to use your mind and body in the same way they do, you can duplicate their results.

Have you ever noticed yourself putting your hand on your hip when talking with a friend who has his hand on his hip . . . or folding your arms if she has her arms folded . . . or the husband and wife who laugh in the same way? These are examples of an unconscious process called *mirroring*, one way of modeling someone's behavior. We tend to imitate people we like.

A basic premise in NLP is that by modeling the states of people who are successful in doing something we would like to do, we can get the same results. For physiology we observe how they hold themselves, physical gestures, and mannerisms. For IR's we can study the values, belief systems, and specific mental *keys* they use to get the results they want.

Modeling also shows why it is important to choose friends carefully. If we are around people who consistently complain and indulge in negativity, we are likely to pick up these traits. If we are around happy, successful, and positive people, we are more likely to model these qualities.

Appropriate models provide a clear image of what success really is. The more concrete the image, the more ways our unconscious can program us to achieve the results we want. Being around successful people, watching them on TV, listening to their words, or reading their books provide conscious as well as unconscious strategies to model their success.

LEARNING TO LEARN: THE ADVANTAGE

Our brain functioning style (right brain/left brain) and thinking style (VAK) determine how we think and thus represent the world internally (IR's). Magic keys are the sequence of VAK steps that

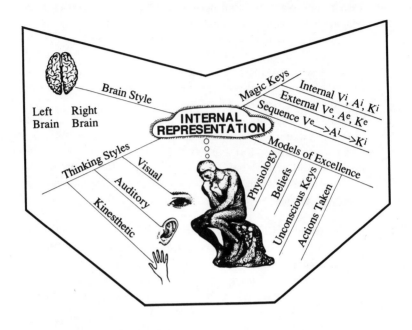

FIGURE 1.1

together with physiology lead to the states we desire. Models provide a shortcut in the process.

My purpose, then, is to provide you with new alternatives to set up states for powerful thinking, for personal power, and especially for learning . . . because achieving your goals or dreams in life will involve learning. As you learn more effectively, you gain *personal power* to achieve your goals, experience the states you like, and have more of those special days.

CHAPTER TWO

Magic Keys:
to direct your
states

Everything should be made as simple as possible, but not simpler.

—ALBERT EINSTEIN

A famous Native American chief in the nineteenth century was asked to comment on the white people and the ingenuity of their emerging technology. His response was that these people were very smart but not wise. Wisdom comes from clarity and simplicity of thought.

Learning to produce desirable states is as simple as understanding how we think—the structure of thought. Two powerful techniques, *pattern discovery maps* and *magic keys*, provide a clear path to navigate from a present state to the more empowering states you desire.

PATTERN DISCOVERY MAPS

In the section following this one we will learn how to direct our states. The strategy to produce a desired state involves steps to change the physiology and steps to change the IR's. The key to changing the IR's is literally that—a *key*, a *magic key*.

Step by step, such a key resembles a recipe or the steps in the laboratory process to produce a certain chemical formula. A useful way to display a particular key is a tool called the pattern discovery map.

EXERCISE 5

Close your eyes for just a few seconds and imagine a car. See the car as clearly as you can, but if you don't see it clearly, that is okay. If you hear it or just sense it, that is also fine. Stop reading until you have completed this.

When you open your eyes, recall where in your field of view the car was located. Was it in the center of your internal field of view? Was it over to one side? Was it above you or below you?"

Most people in my seminars report seeing, hearing, or sensing the car somewhere near the center of the field. That is why a pattern discovery map begins in the center.

Figure 2.1 is an example of a pattern discovery map that summarizes Chapter One. Notice that the main idea is in the center. The most closely related ideas are closest in. From there ideas branch out on lines or curves connected with other lines or curves. This structure parallels the functioning of the right side of the brain in allowing you to see the overall picture of how parts fit together to form the whole.

A pattern discovery map also forms a nonlinear outline. The central topic is in the center. The main headings are closest in. Subheadings branch farther out, and so on.[1]

DIRECTING YOUR STATES

A state such as feeling motivated, focused, in love, or in an appropriate mind-set for learning is a desired outcome, just as a loaf of freshly baked bread is for the baker. Of course, the state may itself be a means toward further outcomes, just as the bread provides nourishment for the day's activities.

A recipe for bread has a sequence of steps we must follow in the proper order. Change the order and we do not get bread.

Achieving a desired state also involves a specific sequence of steps. We begin with physiology, then move through a mental key to direct the IR's.

1, 2, 3, 4 NOT 2, 1, 4, 3

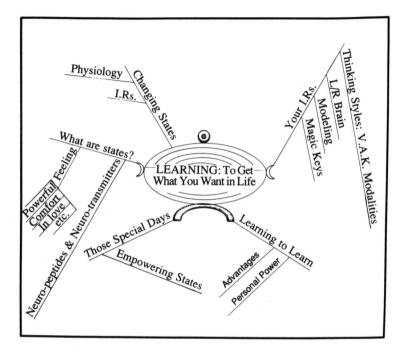

FIGURE 2.1

Adjusting physiology may involve the following:

- a few minutes of physical stretching
- having appropriate lighting, temperature, and back support;
- dietary considerations
- mimicking gestures and mannerisms of someone you would like to model
- just imagining how you would be sitting or standing right now if you were already in the state you desire

We will cover specifics of physiology throughout this book.

The heart of the recipe, though, is the magic key—the sequence of visual, auditory, and kinesthetic, internal and external experiences that lead to the desired state. A notation for *external* stimuli is V^e, A^e, and K^e, where *e* means external. *Internal* experiences—what we "see," "hear," and "feel" inside our heads—are designated V^i, A^i, and K^i, where *i* means internal. Thus if your key for getting started in the morning is to *see* the clock, *hear* a voice inside telling you why you need to get up now and what you have to do, and finally *feeling* inside that you are ready to get up, we can write the sequence as V^e—>A^i—>K^i. A pattern discovery map makes the key more graphic:

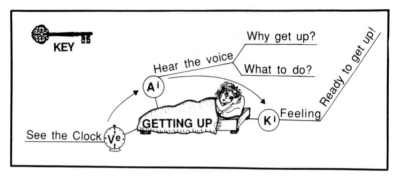

FIGURE 2.2

Visual, auditory, and kinesthetic ways of experiencing are called *modalities* in NLP. These are the ingredients of the recipe, the building blocks of a key. However, a recipe also has directions for how much of each ingredient as well as the type needed. These qualifiers of visual, auditory, and kinesthetic experience are called *submodalities*.

EXERCISE 6

Take a few seconds to think about a close friend or relative. Pick someone you can easily picture, someone with a pleasant voice, and someone you feel especially good about. When you picture this person, is he or she

- close up or far away?
- moving or still frame?
- black and white or color?
- large or small?

EXERCISE 6 (continued)

These qualities are examples of *visual submodalities*. Next, when you think about that person's voice, is it

- loud or soft?
- fast-paced, slow-paced, or in between?
- inflected or more monotone?

These are examples of *auditory submodalities*. Finally, when you think of feelings you associate with this person, which if any of these adjectives feels appropriate?

- warm or cool?
- smooth or coarse?
- firm or soft?
- light or heavy?

These are a few examples of *kinesthetic submodalities*. Submodalities provide power and precision to visual, auditory, or kinesthetic steps in a magic key.

The clock you see in the morning might seem fuzzy, dim, and far away. The voice inside your head telling you to get up might sound fast-paced, high-pitched, and perhaps have a scolding, abrasive, tonal quality. The feeling that you finally have to get up may seem heavy and rough. The completed key then looks like this:

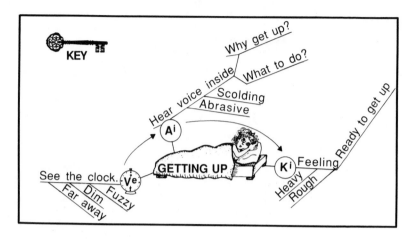

FIGURE 2.3

VISUAL SUBMODALITIES

The following are possible qualities of images you see inside (V^i):

- distance—close up or far away
- color or black and white
- moving or still frame
- bright or dim
- location of image in your field of vision
- associated/disassociated; are you in the scene or an "outside" viewer?
- size—large or small
- sharp focus or fuzzy
- panorama or narrow view
- moving quickly or slowly

AUDITORY SUBMODALITIES

Here are some possible qualities of internal self-talk—voices you might hear inside (A^i):

- high pitch or low pitch
- loud or soft
- tone of voice
- rhythm of speech
- uniqueness of sound (gravelly, smooth, raspy, breathy, etc.)
- your voice or someone else's
- pace of voice
- inflected, resonant, or more monotonous
- length of pauses
- location of sound

In addition to these qualities of what you hear, notice specifically what the voice is saying and if it is critical and demanding or helpful and supportive.

KINESTHETIC SUBMODALITIES

Here are some possible qualities of feelings you experience inside (K^i):

- softness/hardness
- rough or smooth
- a sense of pressure
- tingly
- sharp or dull
- warmness or coolness
- heavy or light

```
------------------------------------------------
|                                                |
|        KINESTHETIC SUBMODALITIES (continued)   |
|                  _____                   |
|                                                |
|                                                |
|     • location of feelings in your body        |
|     • a sense of movement                      |
|     • a sense of tension or melting relaxation |
|                                                |
------------------------------------------------
```

STATE 1: MOTIVATION

Diane had always procrastinated when it came to studying French. She felt overwhelmed at the thought of learning all the details of this language. Her parents had moved from Quebec to New England when she was a baby. They had tried to teach her to be bilingual, but Diane was drawn to her English-speaking friends and TV. Recently, however, her best friend offered to pay her way to France, so they could spend a month bicycling through the countryside in the summer—now six months away. Diane was fascinated at how the same language she had labored through in high school and college was now coming so easily. Anticipation of a vacation she had long desired provided the motivation she needed to excel.

We all have times when we are totally motivated to complete a project, prepare for a vacation, or buy a gift to surprise that special someone we've just fallen in love with. At other times it's all we can do just to get out of bed in the morning. The state we call *motivation* is the springboard to the action it takes to achieve our dreams. Does it have to be by chance that sometimes we are motivated and sometimes we aren't?

According to NLP, achieving a state of motivation is something we inherently know how to do. If our own unconscious processes work well, we simply need to discover consciously what it is, and learn to use it when we want. Or we can model strategies employed by highly motivated people.

EXERCISE 7

To discover your own strategy, begin with physiology. When you are totally motivated, how does your body feel? Are you rested? Have you been exercising? What sensations do you feel in your body? How would you be sitting or standing right now if you were totally motivated and excited about what you are about to do?

For the IR's you need to discover the sequence of steps—the magic key—you unconsciously use to motivate yourself. You can do this by thinking of a specific time when you were totally motivated and consequently completely effective in what you were doing. Be in touch with all the feelings, sights, and sounds from that particular experience. It is crucial to be in touch with that experience as if it were happening *now*. Here is a seven-step process to construct your key.

1. Once you feel yourself back in the experience of being totally motivated, notice the very first thing that must happen for you to be motivated. Is it something you see (visual external—V^e), something you hear (auditory external—A^e), or something you touch (kinesthetic external—K^e)? Write down this very first step.
2. Next, notice what happens on the *inside* once you have seen, heard, or touched what started your motivation. Do you now visualize something inside, hear some words or self-talk inside, or have some internal feelings (V^i, A^i, or K^i)? Once you are aware of this step, write it down.
3. Once you have seen, heard, or felt something inside, does something else internally or externally need to happen for you to be motivated completely? Write down that step. Continue the process until it feels complete. A typical key may involve two to five steps.
4. After you have listed each step, you might conjure up another time when you were totally motivated. Put yourself back in that situation as if it were happening now, and see if that

EXERCISE 7 (continued)

experience involves the same sequence of steps. This may lead to some refinement in your key.

5. Often the first step in your key will be in your dominant modality. If you are primarily visual, the first step is likely to be something you see, something you hear, etc. The last step in your magic key is likely a kinesthetic internal feeling of knowing you are motivated—perhaps feeling it in your body.

6. Once you are convinced you have the correct sequence of steps, set them up in a pattern discovery map, such as shown in Figure 2.4.

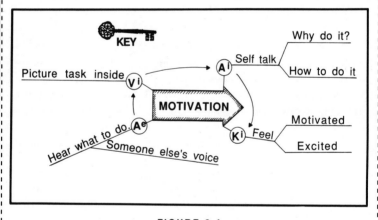

FIGURE 2.4

EXERCISE 7 (continued)

7. Finally, go back over the map and notice one to three of the most important submodalities for each step, especially internal steps. For example, if you hear a voice inside, is the voice stern, monotonous, and quick-paced, or soothing, inflected, and slow? Add submodality qualities to your map as branches from each step. The completed key might then appear as shown in Figure 2.5.

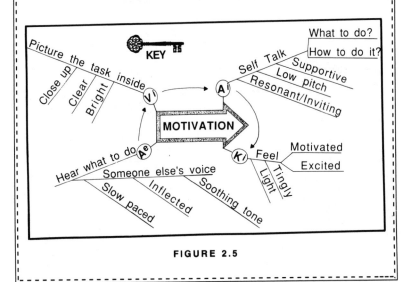

FIGURE 2.5

Exercise 7 is a powerful way to discover how you naturally motivate yourself. Yet another question you might consider is: How effective is your key? Can you easily get yourself motivated when you decide it is important, even if the task is unpleasant? Or do you often procrastinate and feel overwhelmed when thinking about what you need to do?

NLP researchers[2] have studied people who easily motivate themselves as well as people who have much difficulty getting motivated. They find people with motivation problems often taking a negative approach. Such a person might start out *seeing* that marketing presentation she needs to prepare. This may be followed by *hearing* an internal voice scolding in an unpleasant tone, telling why she *has to* do it or what she *should* do. Next, she might feel rebellion: "No, I don't want to do that!" Finally, she visualizes failing and feels terrible at that prospect. Motivation for these people is an attempt to rebel against an inner voice of authority, yet avoid the negative consequences of what would happen if they don't succeed. Since we are rarely attracted to negativity and potential failure, such a strategy leads to internal conflict and procrastination.

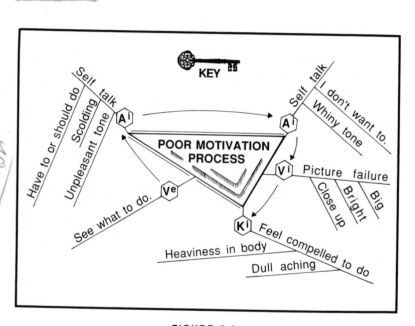

FIGURE 2.6

People who are effective self-motivators generally have positive steps in their keys. They might see what needs to be done, hear supportive and encouraging self-talk on how they can achieve their goal, visualize themselves being successful, and feel how good it will be to complete what they want.

EXERCISE 8

To see how your own self-talk affects you, try the following. Think of a project you really need to do. Imagine a voice inside telling you that you *have to* or *should* do it. How do you feel?

Now change the tone to a soft, soothing, and sexy voice inviting you to start. How do you feel now?

If you don't already have one, you can acquire a powerful motivation strategy simply by changing from a negative to a positive viewpoint (see, hear, and feel success) and by changing the submodalities of each step. So instead of a fast-paced, scolding, authoritative voice telling you what you *have to do*, imagine a soft, sexy, soothing voice inviting you to start a rewarding project. Instead of visualizing a scene of failure in black and white, somewhat out of focus, and at a distance, you might picture a scene of success in color, close up, and in clear focus. Instead of feeling the painful sensations of failure, you might imagine the most important submodalities associated with achieving what you want, perhaps feeling warm, tingly, and light.

Thus positive modalities and compelling submodalities provide the magic of keys and precision of thinking.

Try it.

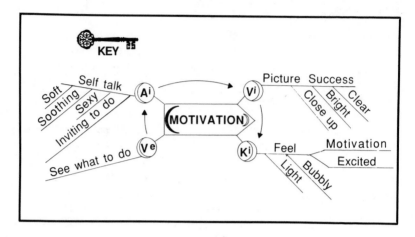

FIGURE 2.7

CHAPTER THREE

*B*RAIN STATES:
HOW YOUR BRAIN
WORKS

When we look into the animal kingdom, we might think of a centipede as a leg specialist . . . an elephant as a nose specialist . . . a giraffe as a neck specialist. But what about us as human beings? We are *brain* specialists, with a highly overdeveloped cerebral cortex.

One way to accelerate learning is to restructure the learning process to parallel the way our brain functions, instead of trying to force our brains to work the way someone else has structured education. There is a big difference here. By knowing how our brain works, it is easier to change our IR's to create a resourceful state for learning.

THE BRAIN'S POTENTIAL

The human brain weighs about three and a half pounds and contains about ten billion cells. Each of these brain cells or neurons may have thousands of fibers or dendrites branching away. The dendrites provide a network of communication pathways among the brain cells. If your brain cells were connected end to end to form a chain, the chain would be a thousand miles long. However, if the dendrites were connected end to end, that chain would be a hundred thousand miles long.

The communication capacity among brain cells is awesome. It is

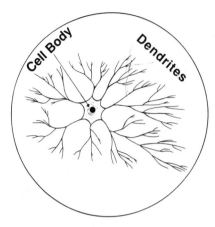

FIGURE 3.1

estimated that a chunk of brain material the size of a pea has the communication capacity of the entire world's telephone systems.[1] The interconnections possible within one human brain are calculated to be greater than the total number of atoms in the universe.[2] In fact, the brain is the most complex creation we are aware of in the universe.

The brain processes a thousand bits of information per second and interfaces with an amazing sensory system. We can perceive as few as a couple of photons of light, or enjoy a sunset, which is ten million times brighter. We can enjoy a live concert or hear corn growing on a quiet day in Kansas (about a billionth as loud as the concert).

With all this potential, you might wonder why people have trouble spelling "onomatopoeia," or working with computers, or having successful relationships. You would think we should all be supergeniuses.

WHAT'S HOLDING US BACK?

There are five major blocks to making full use of our mental potential:

1. *Learning blocks.* For most of us, our internal representations include stress-related barriers to learning. A "learning block" is a stress-related belief: for example, thinking that I can easily spell, but can't do math; or maybe I can be financially successful, but fail at relationships. These limitations are generally based on stressful learning experiences growing up—experiences with parents, teachers, and friends. In certain areas we just don't expect to excel.

EXERCISE 9

Take a minute or two to write a list of the types of learning you find most difficult, frustrating, or blocked for you. These can include sports, manual dexterity, social skills, etc., as well as academic learning. Stop reading until you have completed this.

Once you have this list written down, go back over the items and ask yourself which of these you like to change and which you have no interest in changing.

---

2. *Left-and right-brain learning.* Most education and training is directed primarily to only half of our brain: the left half. That doesn't mean the right half is not working; it certainly is. However, in most learning situations we have an imbalance between the left and right sides of the brain. A better balance would facilitate both learning and memory.

3. *Linking the conscious and the unconscious.* Many researchers believe that we have a supermemory already. Everything that happens during our lifetime is recorded somewhere. The problem is not one of remembering but rather *recalling* what is already there. We can do this by setting up consistent, reliable links with our unconscious.

4. *Development of brain cells.* You've probably heard psychologists say that we use only 5 to 10 percent of our mental potential. Only 5 to 10 percent of our brain cells are fully developed[3] in terms of the interconnections a brain cell, or neuron, can make with other neurons. The average neuron has five to ten dendrites, yet some develop thousands of these communication lines.

The number of brain cells is fixed, but the number of interconnectors increases as we learn more and make better use of our brain. The complexity of the brain and our corresponding intelligence seem to be functions of these interconnectors.

If only 5 to 10 percent of our neurons are fully developed, that means 90 to 95 percent of our brain cells are virtually undeveloped. Many of these virtually undeveloped cells will die off before they can mature. In fact, if you are over thirty and if it has taken you forty minutes to read this book so far, you may have lost 125 brain cells during this time. But don't be alarmed! It's not the book's fault; this is a natural process. You've got another 10 billion cells to go, so you won't run out soon.

If you think of the complexity among 5 to 10 percent of our brain cells vs. what might be possible among all the cells, we're not actually using 5 to 10 percent of our potential. We're probably not using a hundredth of our potential. We may not even be using a thousandth of what might be possible. Certain activities, such as learning and mental exercise, actually speed up the development of neurons, so this is another advantage of improving our learning skills.

5. *No reliable means to direct our states.* As we discussed in Chapter One, learning is a means to experience empowering states, and empowering states are means to accelerate learning.

RIGHT AND LEFT SIDES OF THE BRAIN

The human brain is shaped like a large walnut. The left half of the brain controls the right side of the body (more or less from the neck down), and the right half controls the left side. There is also connecting tissue in between called the *corpus collosum*, which allows information to go back and forth.

We have known for a long time that in most people (not everyone) the left brain is primarily responsible for language. What the right brain does—besides controlling the left side of the body—was a mystery for many years. In fact, some people began wondering whether the right brain was even necessary for higher mental functioning.

During the 1960s Dr. Roger W. Sperry conducted a series of classic experiments at Cal Tech at Pasadena to shed light on the mystery; they earned him a Nobel prize in 1981. In cases of severe epilepsy, surgeons sometimes sever the corpus collosum of the patient. This prevents seizures from spreading from one half of the brain to the other. However, in these "split brain" patients, information can no longer go back and forth between left and right, so it becomes easier to isolate what each side does.

On the surface, a split-brain person appears quite normal. Dr. Sperry discovered that while the left brain in most people is primarily

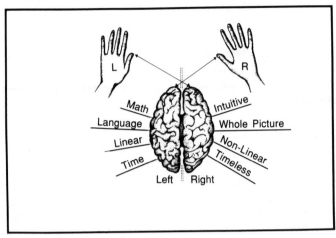

FIGURE 3.2

responsible for language, the right brain deals with feelings and emotions. You might say the left handles what we say, and the right handles the inflections and feelings of how we say it.

The right brain deals with pictures, dreams, and images, while the left has the ability to put those images into words. The left deals with logic, computers, and mathematics, while the right brain deals with math anxiety and computer anxiety—the emotional side of learning blocks. The left brain deals with *linear* thought—putting things into sequence and lists, handling one step at a time. The right brain is nonlinear and works more with parallel processing. It can handle many details simultaneously, such as recognizing a person's face or pulling together the details of a puzzling problem, as when we have a flash of intuitive insight and "see the whole picture." The left brain is aware of the passage of time and helps to keep life organized, sensible, and on schedule. The right brain is more spontaneous and timeless.

We can clearly see the specialization of the left and right hemispheres in accounts of what happens when one side is damaged. A thirty-nine-year-old school teacher with right-brain damage from a stroke found her voice flat and monotonous. Without the emotional content in her voice, she could not maintain classroom discipline. At home when she "meant business" with her children, she had to say in a mechanical tone, "God dammit, I mean it!"

In contrast, a nun sustained left-brain damage from a robber. She was not allowed to testify in her attacker's trial because of her loss of judgment and memory for left-brain sequential detail. She might have identified the attacker in court by walking over and hugging him.[5]

The left-brain/right-brain model also ties in with visual, auditory, and kinesthetic learning styles. The left brain (in most people) deals with words and auditory information. The right brain handles internal visual imagery and kinesthetic feelings.

EXERCISE 10[6]

Sit comfortably and clasp your hands together with the fingers interlocked. Notice which thumb is on top. If the left thumb is on top, this may indicate a left-brain dominance, even though the right brain controls the left side of the body. If the right thumb is on top, this could indicate a right-brain dominance.

In administering right-brain/left-brain testing to over ten thousand seminar participants, I have found a slight statistical tendency for the thumb on top to correlate with brain dominance, although the testing is certainly more accurate than the thumb method.

Stage hypnotists in the past would often have people clasp their hands together like this before inviting someone to come onto the stage. They made sure to invite someone who had the right thumb on top. Those people were more suggestible.

LIMITATIONS OF THE MODEL

Nineteenth-century researchers noted that left-brain damage seems to have more detrimental effects than right-brain damage, probably because we as a society prefer left-brain functioning. Nevertheless, this led to the opinion that the left brain is dominant and the right brain less evolved or advanced. Certainly this is not the case.

At this point you might have the feeling that some activities involve only the left brain and others only the right. This is not so. No matter what you do, both sides participate to some extent. For example, you might be working a crossword puzzle or balancing your checkbook—primarily left-brain activities, but the right brain is still involved. I don't know if you ever notice having emotions when you balance your checkbook. If you are drawing or doing a dramatic performance (primarily right-brain activities), the left brain is still involved.

The specializations of left and right are a *preference*, and when necessary either side can do functions normally associated with the other (to some extent). In fact, in a small minority of people the roles of right and left are entirely reversed (possibly if you are left-handed and your mother was also left-handed). In any case, we need to avoid too-rigid distinctions between left and right.

MEMORY, THINKING, AND LEARNING STATES

When we learn new material, memory of *words* is stored in the left brain, while memory of pictures and images is stored in the right brain.* Thus, when you meet a person, hear the name (left-brain memory), and see the face (right-brain memory), what stays with you longer, the name or the face? Most everyone says the face.

Throughout history, philosophers and writers have speculated about a dual nature of being human. The right brain/left brain model certainly support this view because there are, in fact, two distinct ways of thinking: rational, logical, reasoning states (left brain) and creative, intuitive, emotional thinking (right brain).

Often, however, the highest level of genius involves an appropriate balance between left and right. Many people would think of Einstein as being a classic left-brain scientist, yet he described his discoveries more in terms of right-brain intuitive states.

While riding a trolley to work at the patent office in Switzerland, he would observe the town clock and daydream, "How would the world appear to a beam of light leaving that clock?" Such *Gedanken* or thought experiments led to his theories of relativity.

---

*This can be reversed. A good storyteller uses words (left brain) to create images that you remember more from the right brain. You may see a picture of a car (right brain) and think the word "Chevrolet," which is remembered in your left brain.

THE HUMAN BRAIN VS. COMPUTERS

Computers for the most part simulate left brain thinking: logical, linear, step-by-step, serial. Their usefulness, of course, is in processing large amounts of left-brain data much more quickly and painlessly than we can.

In its way of thinking, the right brain is far beyond computers. It can process thousands of different functions simultaneously with continual cross-referencing and integration of new material. The right brain's ability to do a simple task such as recognizing a face from virtually any angle in less than one second would be an awesome feat for a computer.

Computers also seem unable to handle metaphors or leaps of intuition so commonplace for the right brain. In one experiment,[7] computers translated English to Russian and back to English. When given the phrase "The spirit is willing, but the flesh is weak," what came back was, "The wine is agreeable, but the meat has spoiled." And when given "Out of sight, out of mind," the computer came back with "Blind and crazy."

Learners who prefer to function more from left-brain states tend to master specific details before moving to general relationships. Most formal education favors the linear step-by-step approach and the structure a left-brain learner craves.

Right-brain learners prefer to grasp broad general relationships before proceeding to finer details and specifics. They do well learning in parallel—learning a number of ideas and concepts at once if it isn't necessary to master one topic before proceeding to the next. Also, right-brain learners often do well with unstructured, independent study.

FOUR INFAMOUS FABLES
ABOUT LEARNING[8]

At five years old, Janet could hardly wait to start school. She had so many questions her friends and parents couldn't answer. She loved to learn new skills and ideas. Her brother and sisters got to meet with people called *teachers*. She thought surely these people must have magical powers and adventurous stories to tell.

At age twenty-one, Janet could hardly wait for her last college courses to be over. Learning was drudgery. She had long ago stopped asking most of her questions except "How many units do I need to graduate?" and "Where should I look for a job?" Through her sixteen years of schooling, she had picked up a large body of knowledge, but at a high price. She had also picked up some beliefs that could cripple her learning ability for life. See if any of these "fables" tie in with your experiences.

Fable 1: "My memory is poor." The truth is that each of us already has a perfect memory, and as we discussed earlier, the problem is recalling information from our unconscious.

Hypnotists and some psychologists have believed this for many years. However, it was only demonstrated scientifically during the 1960s, at the Montreal Neurological Institute, through Dr. Wilder Penfield's brain surgery experiments. You may be aware that during brain surgery, the patient is often kept awake. Dr. Penfield found that when he stimulated one small spot on the cortex with an electric probe, the patient might suddenly remember a long-"forgotten" scene from elementary school . . . see the children's faces . . . hear the voices . . . and experience the emotions. Stimulating another spot might take the person back a few weeks ago to details of a bridge party.

When Dr. Robert True[9] of the University of Vermont College of Medicine used techniques of hypnotic age regression with adults, he found that 93% of his subjects could correctly identify the day of the week of their 10th birthday. Sixty nine percent remembered the day of the week of their fourth birthday.

FIGURE 3.3

Fable 2: "I'm not very smart. I just wasn't born that way." This is an unfortunate negative belief that shifts responsibility for poor performance from our belief system to our genetic code. Intelligence is much more related to practice and experience than to heredity. Our brains are somewhat like muscles—the more we use them, the better they get. With mental exercise our speed, accuracy, and confidence get better.

The tragedy of believing we are stupid is that the brain is such a superb learning machine, it can learn to act dumb. We can limit our perception to whatever supports our self-defeating beliefs. By believing we are stupid, we not only find lots of evidence to support us, but we also limit ourselves to a life of inadequacy.

It is absolutely essential, then, to have faith and trust in our brain and internal workings. Eric Jensen, author of *Student Success Secrets*, points out that unconsciously our brain knows how to operate over five hundred muscles and two hundred bones. Our heart beats nearly a hundred thousand times per day, pumping sixteen hundred gallons of blood through 60 miles of veins and arteries to each of the billions of cells in our body. The brain itself is the most complex creation we know of in the universe and is more complex than our solar system. The brain is nature's most superb creation—and yours is no less so than anyone else's.

Fable 3: "I just don't have *time* for new learning." Thomas Edison, when asked the secret to his success, responded that he did only one thing at a time. That is probably an oversimplification. More likely he put *full concentration* on one task at a time, while still handling all the other details of his life.

Psychologists tell us that we can keep track of about seven things at once—seven numbers, seven introductions at a party, seven items on a grocery list—without breaking the list down to smaller units. Yet how many of us have only seven things happening in our lives? For most of us life becomes a juggling game. We juggle our seven items, and the other pieces fall on the floor. Then we pick up those pieces, and still others fall. How can we possibly keep on top of all the activities, commitments, and interests in our sphere of influence?

Later we will learn some simple and powerful time-management principles to keep our movement through life balanced. These allow us to "see the whole picture" (right brain) easily and yet focus totally on the details at hand (left brain), the way Edison advised.

If you don't have enough time for new learning, you may literally run out of time sooner than you hope. There is an increasing body of research suggesting that better use of your mind promotes longevity.

Fable 4: "The older you get, the harder it is to learn new ideas and

FIGURE 3.4

skills." This is a most harmful belief, with little basis in fact. The more an aging person believes this, the more evidence they find to support their belief. This vicious circle leads many elderly people to unstimulating lives with few creative or intellectual challenges. It is likely that memory loss is more connected with stress and worry about memory loss than physiological causes.

A number of studies have demonstrated the potential that senior citizens can learn as well as or even better than high school or college students. In one study done by Else Harwood and Geoffrey Naylor[10] at the University of Queensland in Australia, a group of students sixty years or older studied German. In just six months of class (two hours per week plus one hour of homework), most achieved a level comparable to two years of daily classes in high school.

Age, then, is no barrier to better use of our brains. And by understanding the brain's true potential, the right-brain/left-brain specializations, and limiting beliefs holding us back, we are more likely to live up to our role as the brain specialists we are.

----

PART TWO

*S*TATES

OF

*T*HOUGHT

CHAPTER FOUR

Discovering how you think

Brain: brān n: an apparatus with which we think we think.

—*AMBROSE BIERCE*

How do you think? Do you think more in pictures or internal self-talk, or feelings? Are you more intuitive and emotional, or logical and reasoning? Knowing the way you think affects how you can learn most effectively and how you can go about fulfilling your dreams.

This chapter has two tests for determining how you think, together with explanations and interpretations of your styles.

TESTING FOR YOUR BRAIN FUNCTIONING STYLE

This first test is designed to give you information on your internal representations. Do you prefer to function more from the right or the left side of the brain? What is your particular style of functioning? For each question there are four answers.

• number your *best* choice "4"
• number your next-best choice "3"

• number your third choice "2"
• number your last choice "1"

For example if you rated responses to question #1 like this:

1. _____

   _3_ a.
   _4_ b.
   _2_ c.
   _1_ d.

your top choice would be "b" and your last choice "d." Work quickly, and go with the first feelings of your preference.

BRAIN PREFERENCE AND STYLE INVENTORY[1]

- -

1. New ideas are true for me if
   ____ a. they reflect my values and ideals.
   ____ b. they are scientific and logical.
   ____ c. I can personally verify them with observable facts.
   ____ d. they are in line with my own experience and opinions.

2. My memory is best for
   ____ a. mainly general ideas with some specific details.
   ____ b. mainly specific details.
   ____ c. mainly specific details with some general ideas.
   ____ d. mainly general ideas.

3. Rate your preference for the following *types* of activities:
   ____ a. camping, dancing, or tennis.
   ____ b. writing, collecting, or chess.
   ____ c. reading, playing a musical instrument, or home improvement.
   ____ d. swimming, doing nothing, or a leisurely walk.

4. My planning for the day usually involves
    ____ a. imagining the people I want to see and things I want to do.
    ____ b. listing out things to do.
    ____ c. making a schedule of activities with priorities and perhaps a time frame for each.
    ____ d. just letting the day unfold as it will.

5. To solve a difficult problem, I prefer to
    ____ a. go for a walk to think about it and then talk with others.
    ____ b. think it over and analyze the options on paper.
    ____ c. tackle the problem with approaches that worked for similar past problems.
    ____ d. do nothing and see if the problem will solve itself.

6. Rate how the following pairs of statements relate to you:
    ____ a. I am very much in touch with my feelings, *and* I like to let someone else take charge in group or team activities.
    ____ b. I control my feelings well, *and* I would rather let someone else take charge in group or team activities.
    ____ c. I control my feelings well, *and* I like to take charge in group or team activities.
    ____ d. I am very much in touch with my feelings, *and* I like to take charge in group or team activities.

7. I can estimate pretty accurately the amount of time that has passed without checking a clock
    ____ a. rarely.
    ____ b. often.
    ____ c. sometimes.
    ____ d. hardly ever.

8. In my spare time I would rather read about
    ____ a. how someone solved a social or personal problem.
    ____ b. historical or scientific research.
    ____ c. a true-life adventure or experience.
    ____ d. an interesting or humorous story.

9. With regard to intuition or hunches
    ____ a. I have strong hunches and sometimes follow them.
    ____ b. I don't go on hunches when it comes to important decisions.
    ____ c. I sometimes have hunches but usually don't trust them.
    ____ d. I often have strong hunches that I act on.

10. My mood goes through frequent swings
    ____ a. sometimes.
    ____ b. not true.
    ____ c. rarely.
    ____ d. often.

11. Which activities best describe you? I
    ____ a. am good at reading diagrams or listening to another's feelings.
    ____ b. am good at reading contracts or taking detailed notes.
    ____ c. enjoy chatting or can have difficulty operating mechanical devices under stress.
    ____ d. strongly visualize the setting and characters in stories I read or am good at creating innovative ideas.

12. Which best describes you? I am
    ____ a. caring.
    ____ b. orderly.
    ____ c. practical.
    ____ d. intuitive.

13. When speaking with others I
    ____ a. sometimes make up metaphors or stories.
    ____ b. use a clear, precise choice of words.
    ____ c. sometimes make up puns.
    ____ d. sometimes make up new words.

14. When it comes to adhering to rules or policy, my attitude is
    ____ a. Question authority.
    ____ b. Follow the rules.
    ____ c. Rules and policies usually allow for the best results.
    ____ d. I would just as soon break the rules as follow them.

15. For the following, rate yourself on a scale from 1 to 4. Circle the number that best fits you.

1 ——————— 2 ——————— 3 ——————— 4

| I prefer to master one of two areas of learning rather than spread myself thin. | I would rather know a little bit about many different subjects. |

- If you circled 1, record: 4 for b, 3 for c, 2 for a, 1 for d.
- If you circled 2, record: 4 for c, 3 for b, 2 for a, 1 for d.
- If you circled 3, record: 4 for a, 3 for d, 2 for c, 1 for b.
- If you circled 4, record: 4 for d, 3 for a, 2 for c, 1 for b.

____ a.
____ b.
____ c.
____ d.

16. My attitude about daydreaming is that it
    ____ a. can be useful in solving problems.
    ____ b. is a bad habit.
    ____ c. is amusing but not very practical.
    ____ d. is a valuable technique for planning.

17. When learning new material I would rather
    ____ a. be spontaneous and flexible in my approach to learning and study with some specific planning or directions.
    ____ b. follow closely a specific schedule or action plan for learning.
    ____ c. follow a specific plan with flexibility and leeway.
    ____ d. not be tied down to any particular plan for learning.

18. When getting together socially with others I
    ____ a. occasionally like to be spontaneous.
    ____ b. definitely prefer activities that are planned in advance.
    ____ c. usually prefer activities that are planned in advance.
    ____ d. prefer to be spontaneous.

19. The following are most true for me:
    ____ a. I remember directions and facts by visualizing, and I prefer security to risk-taking.
    ____ b. I remember directions and facts best by writing them down, and I prefer more certainty to risk-taking.
    ____ c. I remember directions and facts best by writing them down, and I am willing to take risks.
    ____ d. I remember directions and facts by visualizing, and I enjoy taking risks.

20. When people argue over some point, I favor the one who
    ____ a. reflects my ideals and values.
    ____ b. is most logical and orderly.
    ____ c. delivers the arguments in a practical, forceful manner.
    ____ d. agrees with my personal opinions.

When you are finished, add up the numbers for each of the "b" choices. For example, if this were your test:

1. _____
    _2_ a.
    _4_ b.
    _1_ c.
    _3_ d.

2. _____
    _4_ a.
    _2_ b.
    _1_ c.
    _3_ d.

3. _____
    _1_ a.
    _3_ b.
    _4_ c.
    _2_ d.

Add the *4* from the b on question #1
with the *2* from the b on question #2
with the *3* from the b on question #3, etc.

Once you have completed this, add the "c" scores (e.g., 1 from question 1 plus the 1 for question 2, etc.). Do the same for the "a's" and the "d's":

Total of numbers next to "b" responses _____
Total of numbers next to "c" responses _____
Total of numbers next to "a" responses _____
Total of numbers next to "d" responses _____

The sum of these four numbers should be 200.

Next, record your results in Figure 4.2 (or in a copy of Figure 4.2 if you wish). Where it says "sum of 'b' scores," put a dot *on that line* opposite the scale. Where it says "sum of 'c' scores," again put a dot on that line across from the scale, and so forth for the "a" and "d" scores.

Finally, if you connect the dots with lines, you will create your profile. Here is one reader's profile as an example.

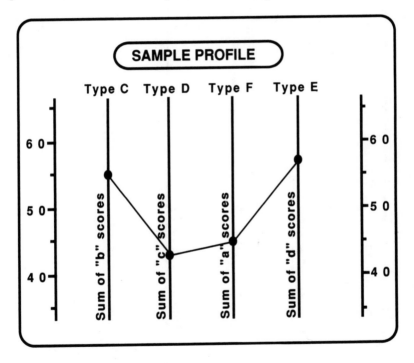

FIGURE 4.1

Stop reading until you have added your scores and recorded them.

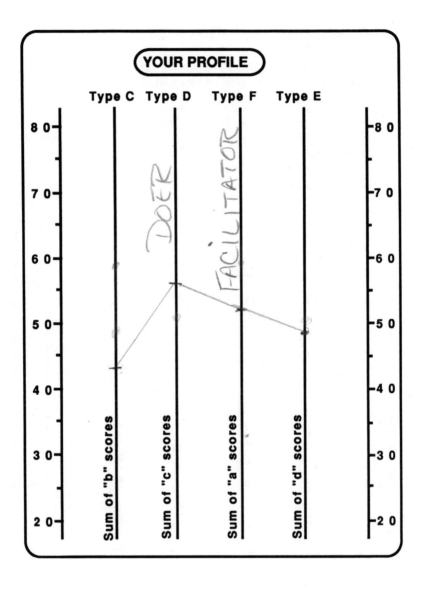

FIGURE 4.2

INTERPRETING YOUR PROFILE[2]

Notice that if your highest score is on the first line (sum of b's), you will be a *type C* individual (see the top of the chart). If your highest score is on the second line (sum of c's), you are a *type D*. If your highest score is on the third line, you are a *type F*, and on the fourth, a *type E*. What do these types mean?

Type C = cerebral. The cerebral person prefers to function very much from the left side of the brain. Cerebral people tend to be quite articulate, but sometimes more flat and unexpressive than other types. They are generally very meticulous and good with detail.

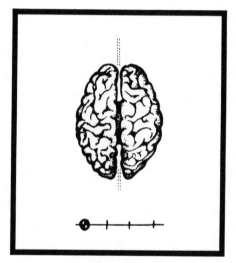

FIGURE 4.3

Dr. Sharon Crane points out in her professional presentation seminars that a cerebral person doing a wallpapering project would probably start in the closet to perfect the skills. Then, when he or she did the walls, the seams would line up perfectly. A past president who was probably a cerebral type was President Richard M. Nixon, an outstanding debater.

Cerebral people are sometimes more formal and reserved than other types. They may not do well with criticism because they want to be perfect. Their strength lies in the high standards they set for themselves and their attention to detail.

Type D = doer. The doer prefers to function moderately to the left side of the brain. The doer type tends to be articulate like the cerebral but more expressive. They are often "bottom line" and results-oriented.

They are good at getting things started and moving—hence the term "doer"—although they may not always complete things.

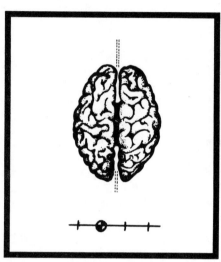

FIGURE 4.4

Doers have a high ego strength and are decisive, competitive people. In contrast with the cerebral, who will often listen a great deal to take in data, doers may not listen well. They usually have their own ways of doing things.

Again, Dr. Crane points out that a doer working with wallpaper would probably start at one end of the room and work straight across. If a seam didn't line up, he or she might cover it with a picture. President Lyndon Johnson, who was strongly results-oriented, was most likely a doer. President Ronald Reagan was probably also in this category, although he was likely a combination of types.

The doer's strength lies in his or her ability to get things moving—which is often the hardest step in an activity.

Type F = facilitator. The facilitator tends to function moderately from the right side of the brain. They generally are more people-oriented and sensitive to feelings than the left-brain types. They often listen more than they speak and thus make good counselors. A facilitator doing a wallpaper project would probably do it in such a way as to please other people—that is, ask others how they wanted it done. A past president who was very much a facilitator, as I'm sure you can imagine, was President Jimmy Carter, a people-pleaser.

Facilitators often crave security. Their strength lies in their ability to be holistic thinkers (seeing the whole picture), and they often work well in groups.

Type E = expressive. The expressive type tends to function far from the right side of the brain. They are often very humorous, colorful, spontaneous, and outgoing with people. Their talking and ways of doing things may seem disorganized to others, but they have their own means of order. They are sometimes drawn to flashy clothes and cars.

An expressive doing a wallpaper project might choose bold color combinations and patterns. President John F. Kennedy was most likely an expressive. President Reagan was probably a combination of doer and expressive.

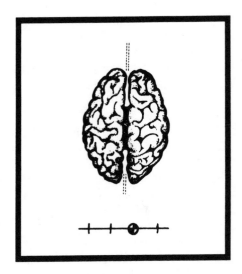

FIGURE 4.5

If your top two scores were within three or four points of each other, you might be one of the following combinations:

Doer and facilitator. This is what Wonder and Donovan in *Whole Brain Thinking* refer to as a *mixed dominant*—a little left and a little right. This is an ideal pattern for a manager, who needs to be "bottom line"- and results-oriented but also good with people and feelings. The mixed dominant can *simultaneously* attend to left-brain detail *while* maintaining the whole picture. This is also useful in new learning.

A problem can occur with this type if one side of the

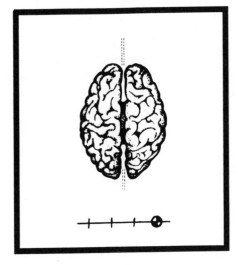

FIGURE 4.6

brain does not clearly dominate.[3] Then you might feel like you have two competing voices within, pulling you in different directions. The result can be dyslexia or stuttering. However, this problem is rare, and the mixed dominant type is generally a good learning combination.

Cerebral and expressive. This combination is called high lateral—you can function very much from the left brain *or* very much from the right brain, but not both at the same time. This type is more common with men. The classic example is the accountant during the day who comes home and spends the evening swimming or dancing . . . or Einstein, who spent his spare time daydreaming or playing the violin.

Cerebral and doer. This basic left-brain combination is described by Dr. Crane as being potentially one of the most dynamic productive combinations. The doer gets things moving, and the cerebral handles fine details. She also describes this as potentially one of the most stress-producing combinations. The doer wants to get things done quickly, while the cerebral demands a perfectionist slowness. The key here is an appropriate balance between these two tendencies.

Facilitator and expressive. This is a fairly frequent right-brain combination. When you read characteristics of the facilitator and the expressive types, you will probably find some of each that apply to you.

Cerebral and facilitator or doer and expressive. These combinations are a bit more unusual. Frequently, a person who prefers right-brain functioning takes on left-brain skills to get a job. When it comes to employment, our society strongly favors left-brain skills. When you look in the want ads, how many times do you see an ad for a poet . . . or a philosopher . . . or a fine artist? Instead, the ads are usually for engineers, accountants, technicians, and clerical workers, whose work demands primarily left-brain skills.

Another possibility for these combinations is a person who prefers left-brain functioning but has added right-brain skills to deal with people and feelings or right-brain problem-solving strategies. A classic example is the engineer who is promoted to management.

LIMITATIONS OF THIS TESTING

You will notice that you didn't score 0 on any of the types. We are each a combination of all four, and you may have noticed characteristics in you from each category. In most situations, however, we tend to function primarily in one or two modes.

When I do this testing in my seminars, most people feel that the description of their type pretty closely matches their own self-image. That's not to say that the test is foolproof. Clinical psychology testing to determine your brain preference style can go into much more detail.

Also, our mode of functioning can change with time. The results on your test a year from now might be quite different from what they are today. Even with these limitations, however, this test is a fairly reliable quick indicator of your style of thinking.

TESTING YOUR MEMORY AND THINKING STYLE

Following are some questions to determine how you think and remember. The questions are structured similarly to those in the first test you just took.

For each question there are three answers:

3 = your best choice
2 = your second-best choice
1 = your last choice

For example, if you rated responses to question 1 like this:

1. _____
    _2_ a.
    _3_ b.
    _1_ c.

your best choice would be "b," and your last choice "c."

INTERNAL REPRESENTATIONS ASSESSMENT

For each question rate each of the three answers:

3 = your first choice
2 = your second choice
1 = your last choice

Work quickly and go with whatever seems right for you.

1. I most effectively communicate what is happening inside of me
   ____ a. through my tone of voice and choice of words.
   ____ b. through my eyes.
   ____ c. through my posture and the emotions I convey.

2. When I don't quite understand or remember something
   ____ a. it doesn't ring a bell or resonate.
   ____ b. it seems hazy or unclear.
   ____ c. I can't get a handle on it or a feel for it.

3. I most easily notice
   ____ a. the quality of music from a stereo.
   ____ b. if colors or shapes clash.
   ____ c. if clothes feel uncomfortable.

4. When I am fully involved, I am _____ what I am doing.
   ____ a. tuned in with
   ____ b. focused on
   ____ c. in touch with or connected with

5. I express myself best by
   ____ a. speaking my ideas.
   ____ b. describing my picture or vision.
   ____ c. writing my thoughts or expressing my feelings.

6. In a discussion, a person will most quickly get my attention by
   ____ a. their tone of voice and choice of words.
   ____ b. their point of view.
   ____ c. their emotional expressiveness.

7. When I have leisure time I prefer to:
   ____ a. listen to music.
   ____ b. sightsee.
   ____ c. go dancing.

8. An effective way for me to make decisions is to rely on
   ____ a. what resonates or sounds best to me.
   ____ b. what looks clearest to me.
   ____ c. gut-level feelings.

9. Learning academic or technical material is easiest for me when
    ____ a. someone explains the ideas to me.
    ____ b. I visualize the concepts and see the whole picture.
    ____ c. I can learn by doing or get a feel for the ideas.

10. At a party, I am most attracted to people who
    ____ a. are interesting, articulate speakers.
    ____ b. radiate visual beauty.
    ____ c. convey a warm, relaxed feeling.

11. The most important thing to help me remember directions is to
    ____ a. repeat them to myself as I hear them.
    ____ b. visualize them.
    ____ c. write them down or intuitively sense how to get there.

12. Once I completely understand a new idea or concept
    ____ a. I have it loud and clear.
    ____ b. I can envision it.
    ____ c. it is now concrete or I have a feel for it.

13. In my environment I am mostly to notice
    ____ a. sounds and quietness.
    ____ b. visual coordination and beauty.
    ____ c. feelings of warmth and/or comfortable furniture.

Once you have finished, add up your scores as you did in the previous test:

- Add up the numbers next to each "b" response. Put the total below.
- Next, add up the numbers next to each "a" response and again put the total below.
- Finally, add the numbers next to each "c" response and record the total.

    Sum of numbers next to "b" responses ____
    Sum of numbers next to "a" responses ____
    Sum of numbers next to "c" responses ____

Now you can plot your results in Figure 4.8 (or in a copy of Figure 4.8 if you wish).

To either side of the page you will see a scale. The first line over to the right of the leftmost scale is the sum of your "b" scores. Put a dot on that line opposite the appropriate position on the scale for the sum of your b's. The next line over is the sum of your "a" scores. Put a dot on that line representing the sum of your "a" scores. The last line is the sum of your "c" scores.

For example, if the sums of your scores were

Sum of numbers next to "b" responses <u>21</u>
Sum of numbers next to "a" responses <u>31</u>
Sum of numbers next to "c" responses <u>26</u>

Your profile would look like this:

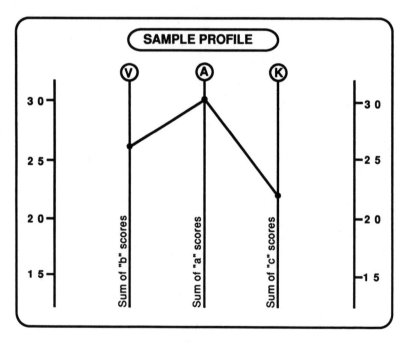

FIGURE 4.7

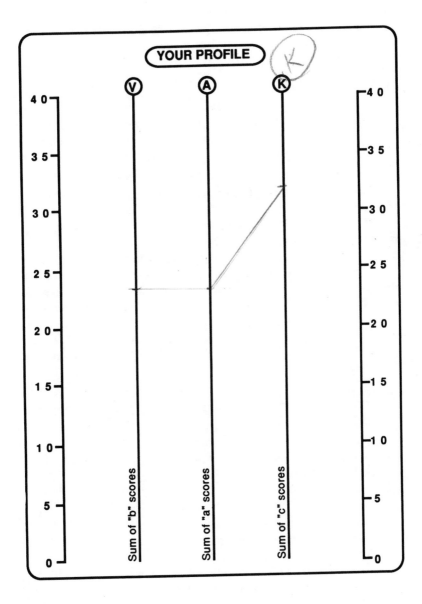

FIGURE 4.8

INTERPRETING YOUR MEMORY AND THINKING STYLE

Once you've charted your results, you'll notice three additional letters, at the top of the chart: "V," "A," and "K." If your highest score is on the first line over, your thinking and memory style is primarily *V*, for visual. If your highest score is on the second line, you are primarily *A*, for auditory. The highest score on the third line over is *K*, for kinesthetic. Here are some general characteristics for each type.

Visuals. Visual people prefer to think, imagine, and remember in terms of pictures or images. They like to look at visual presentations, visualize what they are learning, or see the whole picture. To recall images, most visuals will look up to their left. Some will look up to their right, and a few straight ahead with a glazed appearance as they look inside.

In my seminars I illustrate part of how their strategy works with spelling. I have good spellers come up to the front of the room and give them a difficult word to spell. Inevitably they will look up to the left or more rarely up to the right to remember how the word looks. Such people have evolved an unconscious strategy to "see" the word. English is not always spelled the way it sounds. Looking up is part of accessing that visual image.

EXERCISE 11

To find your direction of visual recall, read each of the following questions and notice which way you naturally look to answer them.

- How many windows are in your house?
- What was the first thing you saw when you woke up this morning?
- Do you remember what your first-grade teacher looked like?
- Which of your friends has the longest hair?

Visual people tend to have an erect posture and breathe from high and shallow in the chest. Their speech is filled with visual references:

- "I see what you mean."
- "Things are looking up."
- "I can picture what you're saying."
- "Today is so bright and clear."

Visuals frequently talk in a high pitch at a fast rate. They see the pictures so quickly, their words can hardly keep pace.

FIGURE 4.9

Auditories. Auditory people think and remember more in terms of sound quality and words. They often learn well by listening or having someone explain something to them.

Talking on the telephone is 100 percent auditory. Think of how you most effectively listen: tilting your head slightly one way or the other and looking straight across toward one side—most likely to your left. Part of the auditory strategy for recall is to look straight across toward the left or occasionally toward the right.

Auditories generally have a more relaxed posture than visuals and breathe more in the middle of the chest. The language of auditories contains phrases like:

- "That really clicks with me."
- "That doesn't ring a bell."
- "It sounds good to me."
- "I hear what you mean."

Auditories speak more slowly than visuals, and the music of their speech is often rich with inflections and intonation. They often take pride in having a resonant voice (e.g., radio announcers and singers).

Kinesthetics. Kinesthetic people involve feelings and tactile sensations in their learning and memory. They often learn by doing or via tactile sensations in their bodies. They need to get a "feel" for the material, make it "concrete," get a "handle" on it. Professional dancers are superb kinesthetic learners.

FIGURE 4.10

To remember feelings and tactile sensations, kinesthetic people will generally look down toward the right or sometimes down toward the left. The posture of a kinesthetic is the most relaxed of the three types, and their breathing is often deep, slow, and from the diaphragm. The language of a kinesthetic often contains phrases like:

- "I'll be in touch."
- "I'm trying to get a feel for how this works."
- "I can't get a handle on it."
- "That guy is such a pain in the . . ."

The speech pattern of a kinesthetic is the slowest of these three types because it takes more time for the kinesthetic to get in touch with his feelings as he is thinking. Once he had grasped a new idea, however, the kinesthetic learner often has a deeper understanding than the other types. Einstein was probably kinesthetic.

EXERCISE 12

To discover the direction you look for kinesthetic recall answer the following questions and be in touch with the feelings described. Notice which way you naturally look to access the feelings . . . down to your left or down to your right.

- Can you imagine how it feels when you are in love?
- Can you imagine the feeling of a nice hot bath or hot tub?
- Can you imagine the feeling of grease covering your hands?
- Can you sense the feeling of movement when you dance freely or participate in your favorite sport?

The direction you look for auditory recall (information you have heard) is likely the same direction (right or left) in which you look for visual recall, except straight across to the side or slightly down. Knowing the directions you naturally look to access visual, auditory, or kinesthetic memories is an important step in learning how to direct your states.

[handwritten margin note: KEEP IN MIND TO CHECK OUT!]

Combinations. Most of us are combination of all three types. You'll notice you didn't score 0 in any one category. We usually have a preference to function from one or two modes, with one or two being weaker or less used. Furthermore, the healthier and more balanced we are, the easier it is to shift our modality to match the task at hand.

If you want to be a good speller or remember the locations of bones and muscles, it is useful to set up a visual state for yourself. If you want to learn music appreciation or a foreign language, an auditory state is more appropriate. For a sport, dancing, or processing emotions, a kinesthetic state works best.

LEARNING, KEYS, AND THINKING

Knowing your preferred modality or modalities connects with learning and magic keys. Most of the time you'll do best to have your first exposure in new learning be in your preferred modality. Thus, if you are studying accounting and are primarily visual, your most effective first step might be to read the material or see charts, diagrams, or pictures of how the methods work. If you are auditory, you might do better to start out hearing the instructor or a friend talk about the material, with opportunity for you to discuss it and ask questions. If you are kinesthetic, it may be important for you to write the material down or get "hands on" experience as quickly as possible.

The first step in your unconscious keys for motivation, falling in love, feeling empowered, etc., are also quite often the same as your preferred modality. Beyond the first step, our overall process or key for a particular state or for learning may ultimately involve all three modalities with both external and internal steps.

Our IR's are determined by how we think. Thoughts have structure and building blocks, just as matter is composed of atoms and molecules. Thoughts and beliefs are structured from visual, auditory, and kinesthetic impressions, based on how we are using the left and right sides of the brain. Now that we understand this structure, we are in a better position to direct our thinking.

CHAPTER FIVE

*P*OWERTHINKING

For those who only feel, life is a tragedy.
For those who only think, life is a puzzle.
For those who think and feel,
in the freedom of NOW,
life is a romantic comedy.

—*ANONYMOUS*

The human brain is the most complex creation we know of in the universe. We have the gift of nature's most remarkable engineering feat, but we were not given an instruction manual!

This chapter is a collection of brain stretchers to balance thinking and feeling and thus allow us to shift our states. We contrast left brain vs. right brain thinking, and how to promote visual, auditory, and kinesthetic thinking.

RIGHT-BRAIN AND LEFT-BRAIN THINKING [1]

The ideal situation in learning is an appropriate *balance* between the left and right sides of your brain for learning the task at hand. Remember, too, that learning is not just academic, but covers life in general.

Here is a test of your knowledge of the left and right sides of the brain. We will look at five social situations where one or more people are acting from an imbalance between left and right thinking. Before you read my interpretation, you might take a separate piece of paper and identify what you think the imbalance is in each case.

PROBLEM 1

You and a close loved one are having a totally unproductive argument. You are each caught up in your own (feelings.) Neither is really listening to the other. What do you think the imbalance is?

EMOTIVE Rt. HEMISPHERE

My answer: The two of you are functioning too much from (the right side of the brain)—you are too caught up in your own emotions to deal rationally with the issues or to hear the other person.

One elegant way to shift more toward the left is for the two of you to separate and write a letter to each other. The letter should be a description of what you are feeling, not the issues or put-downs of the other person. Write a vivid description of *how you experience your feelings.* The description should be so graphic and vivid that anyone reading your words will literally be able to taste what you experience: "I feel such intense anger . . . like ropes coiled around my chest and sandpaper burning across my forehead."

By expressing your feelings in written form, what are you doing? You are shifting more toward the left brain to diffuse the feelings. You are certainly not ignoring them. In fact, you are dealing with the feelings first, but in a left-brain way.

When you get together and exchange letters, you taste what the other person experiences. After reading the letter, take a few minutes for each of you to discuss feelings you perceived in the letter and to convince the other you understand the feelings. This step is crucial. Isn't one of the most frustrating things in an argument that the other doesn't know or care about your feelings? Once you have dealt with the feelings in a left-brain way, you can handle the issues more easily.

TRY THIS!

PROBLEM 2

You are working on a detailed problem, start to feel over-whelmed by the amount of detail, and can't see how it fits together. What do you think the imbalance is?

Go RIGHT, YOUNG MAN, Go RIGHT! BACK UP AND see!

TOO INVOLVED !←

My answer: You are too much to the left. You can't see the forest for the trees. You aren't getting the whole picture or perspective.

Here what you need to do is to shift back toward the right. Shortly we will see several techniques to promote that shift. See the "For Right-Brain Thinking" box.

PROBLEM 3

Someone lays into you with heavy criticism. What do you think the imbalance is liable to be?

TOTAL RIGHT - EMOTIONAL ! (ANGER, HURT, ETC)

My answer: Very likely you will shift too far to the right and be caught in your own emotions and defenses. The person criticizing is probably already in that state.

Again, here you need to shift left. Dr. Sharon Crane[2] describes an effective technique called "fogging" to get out of this situation. When the person criticizes you:

1. Repeat back to them the criticism as you understand it. This assures them that you are getting what they are saying.
2. Then ask them, "What *in particular* is the problem here?" Step 2 is what creates the fog, "What in particular" demands that they search out left-brain detail. They initially may not be able to answer the question because they are caught in right-brain feelings. So if they hit you with more criticism, you repeat

steps 1 and 2. If you keep hammering away at "what in particular," they will have to shift left at some point. Now you have diffused the emotions and can get on with the actual issues.

PROBLEM 4

You are sitting in a class or lecture and are completely bored. What do you think the imbalance is?

My answer: Probably *both* sides of your brain are shutting down. Here you must decide if the information is important for you to get. If the material is important, you are obviously not in a resourceful state. What do you do to change your state? By changing your physiology and your IR's, we know that you can get yourself into a more productive state. For your physiology, stretch while you are sitting. Imagine how you would be sitting if you were totally fascinated with the class. Move your body in some way.

To change your IR's you can activate your left brain by taking detailed notes. Even though this might be the most boring material or speaker you can imagine, analyze it to pieces.

To activate your right brain, notice things such as voice inflections or body language. Is there any emotion behind what the speaker is saying? "What does this person really want to say?" "What would this person rather be doing?" Within a few minutes you can completely change your state and get the information you need.

PROBLEM 5

You are talking on the telephone and want to listen carefully to the words and detail spoken. Which ear should you use?

My answer: Above the neck, right and left crossover does not work in exactly the same way as below the neck. However, most of the signals (not all) from the right ear goes to the left brain, and most from the left ear goes to the right brain.

To listen to verbal detail, use the right ear. To listen more to emotional content or what they really want to say, use the left ear. Most of us have a habit of using one ear or the other, so it may feel odd to switch. It's not that by using the left ear you won't get the words or detail, or by using the right ear you won't get the feelings. Information goes back and forth across the corpus callosum in a fraction of a second. It's just that by using your right ear, the first impulse or impression goes to the left brain, and visa versa. As a test, you might listen with one ear, then ask them to repeat the material and listen with the other ear.

STATES OF RIGHT-BRAIN THINKING

This section and the next present some techniques[3] to allow you to shift easily between right-brain and left-brain thinking.

You will want to shift right if you are overwhelmed by details of a problem and want to step back to see the whole picture. If your job and daily activities are primarily left-brain, you can create more balance in your life by spending more time with right-brain activities. As you will see shortly, this also enhances left-brain functioning.

Unlike other states, such as motivation, feeling in love, etc., with a specific set of steps for your physiology and a magic key, right-brain thinking and left-brain thinking are a bit more elusive to establish. Nevertheless, here are some suggestions to promote right-brain thinking.

FOR RIGHT-BRAIN THINKING

- Look for general relationships in material.
- Go for a leisurely walk.
- Spend time drawing or even doodling.
- Allow time for daydreaming, humming, whistling.
- Allow time to be light, playful, and joking.
- Use pattern discovery maps. — *MIND MAPS*

STATES OF LEFT-BRAIN THINKING

You will want to shift left when you are caught up in feelings, such as an argument, criticism, or depression. Or perhaps your daily activities and work are primarily right-brain, but you would like to create more balance in your life.

FOR LEFT-BRAIN THINKING

- Ask detailed questions (e.g., What in particular?).
- Take detailed notes.
- Do outlining and structured writing like the love-letter technique or keeping a personal journal.
- Do crossword puzzles.
- Do math problems.
- Make up puns.
- Break problems up into separate parts.
- Stick closely to a time schedule.*
- Use pattern discovery maps. *MIND MAPS w/ DETAILED SUB-NOTES*

*Right-brain people can be very unaware of time.

MIND MAPS

You'll notice pattern discovery maps in the last two boxes. As we have discussed, this way of organizing material simulates right-brain functioning.

The pattern discovery map is also a beautiful device for balancing right-brain/left-brain thinking. The left brain deals with the words, ideas, and details of the map, while the right brain deals more with the overall pattern—how everything links together and interconnects. This way of organizing material has some big advantages over traditional note-taking or outlining.

HOW TO ENHANCE LEARNING

If you are primarily a doer or cerebral, you will probably learn material best in a left-brain way. You are most effective in a highly structured learning situation and do best one piece at a time. You have the advantage that most formal education favors your learning style.

Your strength is in handling fine detail, and your weakness is in discovering broad, general relationships. When setting up a study plan, you would do well to construct a detailed schedule and action plan for learning and covering the material. Your natural style is to learn specifics first and then put them together in broad, general relationships.

Since left-brain learners often have difficulty discovering broad, general relationships and seeing the whole picture, your study plan includes a good portion of time putting things together. A very useful tool toward this end is to structure the material into a pattern discovery map.

If you are a facilitator or an expressive, you will learn material better in a right-brain way. You have an advantage over left-brain learners in being able to do better in less structured, independent study. Your natural learning style is to discover broad general concepts first and then focus on the details. Where you may fall short is in getting around to all the details.

If you can find several different topics in your study that don't depend on each other, you can learn them at the same time. For example, if you are taking a tennis class, you might study the rules of tennis, execution of strokes, and strategy all at the same time. A left-brain type might prefer to take them in sequence.

In studying a text, you don't need a detailed study plan. Just get moving. Of course, this can be one of the hardest steps. You are spending less time putting things together than left-brain learners, and you need to focus more on picking up the details. It is also valuable for you to organize your notes in pattern discovery maps.

SEXUAL DIFFERENCES

Generally, girls develop language skills earlier than boys. This gives them a head start on left-brain skills. H. T. Epstein[4] has estimated that by age eleven, girls' brains are developing at about twice the rate of boys'.

By spending more early time with right-brain activities, boys usually wind up being better with spatial relationships. By age fifteen their brains are developing about twice as fast as girls'.

Women have a thicker corpus collosum than men. Presumably this provides more nerve fibers connecting left and right—which may account for women seeming more intuitive.

RIGHT-BRAIN/LEFT-BRAIN MEMORY ENHANCERS

The memory of words and verbal detail physiologically is stored more in the left brain, and memory of pictures, images, and spatial relationships is more in the right. The most superior memory however, is one that is simultaneously right brain and left brain *plus a way of connecting the two*. When you did the twenty-term exercise in Chapter One, your first exposure probably resulted primarily in left-brain memory. The second time we added right-brain visual images for the words, plus a story that connected the words with images.

If you were learning the Portuguese word *solteiro* (sohl-tay-ee-roo), meaning bachelor, you could repeat the word and meaning a few times and create an unreliable left-brain memory.

You might, however, notice that this word sounds a little like "salty hero." You could imagine Popeye the Sailor, who is a salty hero and also a bachelor. Again, you have left-brain sounds and words, a right-brain picture, and a connection.

VISUAL THINKING

Improved visual thinking can sharpen your observation skills, promote photographic recall, and provide you with a clear picture of the goals and states you desire. As well, visualization may develop the corpus collosum linking the left and right hemispheres of the brain. Dreams and images are the language of the right. Interpreting and understanding these images is a job for the left. The corpus collosum allows flow of thought back and forth.

Improved visual thinking has three components: improved external visual perception (V^e), modeling the physiology and IR's of the best visual thinkers, and improved internal visualization (V^i). Here are a couple of approaches to enhance visual perception:

- Take a course in drawing. One of the best I've seen is a self-directed course presented in the book *Drawing on the Right Side of the Brain*, by Betty Edwards. Her exercises promote enhanced right-brain functioning and sharpened visual skills, and they are fun. They also provide a great metaphor, because most of us have strong learning blocks when it comes to drawing. To discover that you can draw much better than you thought may open up new possibilities to do other things you didn't think you could do. Furthermore, they promote communication between the left and right hemispheres through the corpus collosum.
- Another approach to sharpen visual perception is to *reverse a familiar scene*. Take a familiar setting, such as your bedroom, office, or front yard, and study it through a mirror. Reversing the images will bring out many mundane details you've seen many times but failed to notice.

We can best model powerful visual thinkers by modeling how they handle their physiologies. If you were such a person you would

- assume a straight, upright posture.
- look in your direction of visual recall to picture something you've seen before.
- look up and to the opposite side to picture something you've never seen before. Thus you may look up to your left to imagine your best friend smiling. However, you would probably look up and toward your right to imagine how you'll look in five years with your first million dollars or to picture yourself with that man or woman of your dreams.

We can illustrate how to model strong visual thinkers' IR's through the *key* most of them unconsciously use to be excellent spellers.

THE MAGIC KEY FOR SPELLING

1. If the word is longer than 5 or 6 letters, break it down into smaller units or chunks (e.g., onomatopoeia—> ono-ma-topoe-ia).
2. Look (V^e) at the whole word for a shorter word or just the first chunk for a longer word, and imagine your eyes and brain are a camera taking a picture of the word.
3. While you are doing this, assume a visual posture and physiology (K^e).
4. Look in your visual direction and visualize the letters (V^i). Some people visualize more clearly with their eyes open, others more clearly with their eyes closed. If you don't "see" the letters, repeat step 2.
5. Trace the letters in the air with your finger (K^e).
6. Look again in your visual direction to see the letters (V^i).
7. Read the letters out loud in *reverse* order (A^e). If you can do this, you have a clear visual image, since English is almost impossible to sound out backward.
8. Do step 2–7 for each chunk of the word, then for the word as a whole. You will experience the feeling (K^i) that you know the word, and with your mental picture, you will never forget the word, just as you are unlikely to forget someone's face.

THE MAGIC KEY FOR SPELLING (continued)

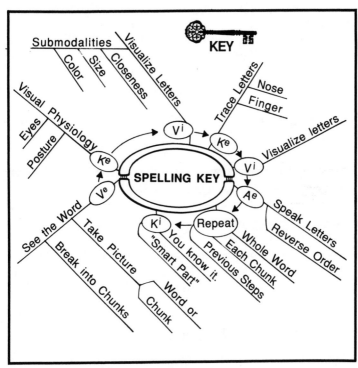

FIGURE 5.1

Most good spellers unconsciously do many of these steps to learn a difficult word. You can further refine the key using submodalities—that is, visualize the letters in your favorite color, or have them be close up or large. With practice the whole process will take only a few seconds.

Exercises to promote internal visualization often start with words (left-brain instructions) such as "imagine yourself lying on the warm sand at the beach . . . staring into a clear, blue sky . . . at a bone-white sea gull gliding in lazy circles." You then convert the words into right-brain images.

Some people get very clear and sharp images, while many people feel frustrated that their images are vague or nonexistent. People frequently ask me at my seminars if there is some way to increase the clarity of their imagery. There are three techniques I can suggest:

1. *Physiology.* Look in your visual direction when you close your eyes. As discussed, this is typically up and to the left for something you've seen before, and up to the right for something you've not seen but want to imagine. You might further imagine (with your eyes closed) that your forehead is a television screen. Look up to see the picture. You may find the imagery more vivid at certain locations.

   Experiment for yourself. You might scan the field from one temple to the other to see where it is clearer. This is what we do in the dream stage of sleep, during rapid eye movement (REM). We look up and scan the visual field—left to right to left.

2. *Sensory overlap.* Some people find it easier to imagine sounds like a running creek or wind rustling leaves in a forest. Others can more easily imagine tactile feelings—walking over the warm sand at the beach or dipping their hand into a cool, rushing creek.

   The procedure here is to start with the sense that you can most easily imagine. As you become absorbed, you may notice visual glimpses of what you are imagining. With practice, those glimpses give way to clearer pictures. In effect, images through one sense enhance production of images through the other senses.

3. *Spontaneous visualization.* This is an innovative third technique, offered by Dr. Win Wenger in *An Easy Way to Increase Your Intelligence.** Instead of trying to force or concoct imagery from the left brain, we simply allow it to occur spontaneously from

*(Gaithersburg, Md.: Psychogenics Press, 1980) pp. 4–7

the right and describe it in words using the left. You can try this out for yourself using the following steps:

- Find a comfortable spot where you can sit undisturbed for ten minutes.
- (Optional) Set up a tape recorder to record your descriptions for future reference and interpretation.
- Close your eyes, relax, take a few deep breaths, and allow any imagery just to happen.
- When imagery comes, describe it aloud in such detail that someone listening would see what you are seeing. Don't label or explain; just describe in vivid detail.
- If imagery is vague, you might look up (with eyes closed) and scan back and forth. Even if it is vague, describe vividly what is there. Often the process of describing it increases the intensity.
- If imagery doesn't come at all after relaxing for a few minutes and looking up, just start describing, aloud, details of a remembered scene or dream. Again, use vivid detail and describe in the present tense, as if it were happening now. As the detail gets finer, you will notice new details streaming in. Just flow with the new imagery, and it will become clearer.

If you practice this procedure ten minutes a day for a few weeks, you should notice a dramatic improvement in your visualization powers. If you want to experience how sharp and clear the imagery can be, do this procedure as you are lying in bed, just starting to fall asleep.*

The crucial factor here is the vivid description in words (left brain). That demands increased functioning of the corpus collosum.

Be patient. Improvement may be slow at first, but your efforts will be rewarded in increasing creativity and the ability to visualize your success.

---

*Rarely some people do not have visual imagery—even during dreaming. They will dream only in sound and feelings. If you "see" things when you dream, you can visualize.

AUDITORY THINKING
- -

"Dammit, you idiot! Can't you get anything right?" Mark blurted to himself as he double-faulted for the second time during the weekend tennis match he plays for fun and recreation. Powerthinking in the auditory mode involves cleaning up such unsupportive self-talk (A^i) as well as refining listening skills (A^e).

Much has been written recently about the detrimental effects of negative self-talk—most of which we may not be consciously aware of. It is well and good to follow the advice of pop psychologists and consciously change the content of self-talk when we become aware we are beating ourselves up internally. The crucial missing piece, however, is taking advantage of *submodalities*. The *qualities* or your inner voice that are most important for you—the pitch, the pace, the resonance, the tone quality, etc.—can have a more profound effect on you than the content.

The external side of auditory thinking is the art of listening. As crucial as careful listening is for classes, relationships, and business transactions, many of us find it difficult to listen carefully. For this reason a purely auditory activity such as talking on the telephone can be quite stressful in long stretches.

The ear is a remarkable sensory detector. The faintest sound the average person can hear is a millionth of a millionth of the loudest sound we can tolerate. Furthermore, the brain has the remarkable ability of filtering out irrelevant sounds, as when a mother can hear the cry of her baby among many in a nursery, or as lovers hear whispered words through the noise of a party.

An important step toward powerful auditory thinking, then, is to sharpen hearing and listening skills. Five approaches are useful here:

1. *Alternate generalized and focused listening.*[4] Focused listening is having your attention on one sound. Generalized listening is allowing your attention to wander. For example, when you are out on a walk, notice what sound or sounds you are focused on—probably that little voice inside your head. Then notice what you are *not* listening to—the sounds of your footsteps, the sound of the afternoon breeze, birds in the background, etc.

You might do the same at a party. Notice the person you are listening to. Then switch to all the other sounds in the room you've been ignoring. This exercise will not only enhance your awareness of the sounds around you but will also reaffirm your confidence in your ability to focus on sounds and to ignore irrelevant sounds.

2. *Model good listeners.* Model the characteristics we discussed in Chapter Four—looking across to one side (most likely your left side), tilting your head as you do on the phone, and assuming a posture slightly more relaxed than the visual one. Of course, in our culture when someone is talking to you, it is considered polite to look at them, but that isn't the best way to hear them. You might explain that what they are saying is really important to you, and to hear them even better you look to the side.

EXERCISE 13

Your direction of auditory recall is most likely straight across on the same side as your direction of visual recall. Verify this for yourself. Listen carefully now to whatever sound is in the background.

1. Look straight ahead and listen as intently as you can.
2. Next, look straight up and listen carefully.
3. Finally, look straight across or slightly down on the same side as your direction of visual recall (probably to the left), tilt your head, and listen. Move your eyes around a little in this position to see where the sound is the clearest.

No doubt you can hear the sounds in all three positions, but which is most comfortable for you? Musicians and people who are quick to pick up foreign languages usually assume the third position.

---

3. *Listen longer.* It is said that wisdom brings us the ability to listen more than we speak. If you are too quick to respond to what

people say, you may be putting more attention on your response than on what they are saying. It is much wiser to make sure they have finished and to verify that you understand what they are saying before launching into your point of view. Even if you disagree, others will feel complimented that they were heard.

4. *Mirror unconscious mannerisms to establish rapport.* Notice a person's submodalities (the pace, inflections, pitch, etc.) and words, and expressions frequently used. Then, *without being obvious*, mimic those mannerisms. This is a very powerful strategy from NLP used in sales to gain unconscious rapport with potential clients. Being in rapport makes it much easier to listen to what they are saying. In a sense you are stepping into their shoes and making it easier for you to see their viewpoint.

5. *Use sensory overlap.* Do this especially when on the telephone or listening to an instructor or trainer who lectures with no emotion or visual aids. While listening, visualize what the person is talking about, and pay attention to feelings or tactile sensations that may be stirred up by what the person is saying.

KINESTHETIC THINKING

Kinesthetic thinking is the ability to access internal tactile sensations and feelings as well as heightened sensitivity to external touch and movement. Champion athletes and professional dancers rank among the best kinesthetic learners. People who are completely in touch with their emotions and "body language" unconsciously practice kinesthetic thinking.

Powerthinking involves being in touch with movement and tactile sensations in a tennis match or with emotions when sorting through a destructive pattern in an intimate relationship. However, powerthinking can just as well involve shifting away from feelings or emotions if they are counterproductive, such as feeling panic during a test or a phobic reaction at the dentist's. Exercise 14 demonstrates some simple shifting into and out of a kinesthetic state.

EXERCISE 14

Think back to a specific time when you were sad or depressed. Be careful to pick an event you feel okay about now so you won't be depressed for the rest of this chapter. Be in touch with the feelings or events as if they were *happening now*.

Next, look down, take a deep breath, slump your shoulders, and intensify your feelings and body sensations. Immerse yourself in that state.

Now sit straight up, put a big smile on your face, look up, and try to be in touch with those sad or depressed feelings. I'll bet you will find it much more difficult to access those feelings in this visual pose. On the other hand, you probably found it easy in the kinesthetic posture.

This exercise provides one method of shifting out of the state called *panic during a test*. When taking a test, you are naturally looking down to answer the questions. If you should start to panic, looking down will perpetuate those feelings. If you simply shift to a visual posture and look up, the panic may subside.

If you watch champion athletes mentally rehearse just before a competition, you will likely see them looking up in their visual direction to see themselves competing in top form. You will probably see them looking down in the kinesthetic direction to remember how it feels to do the winning movements.

Kinesthetic thinking also involves "listening" to your body—that is, being aware of the sensations of how your body reacts to a potential decision or action. For example, if you are thinking of buying a new sports car, your body will react in subtle or sometimes not so subtle ways if you have misgivings—one way or the other. Paying attention to such feelings should not necessarily be the basis of your decision, but it can certainly bring inner conflict to your conscious awareness. Your body does not lie.

At the onset of fatigue, most of us want to run away from the feelings through coffee, diversions, or ignoring the feelings. The next time you feel fatigue, try the opposite approach. By briefly being in touch with your body and its experience of fatigue, you can actively facilitate the body's natural production of neurotransmitters to switch out of that state. On the other hand, the experience may convince you of the wisdom of taking a nap.

Allowing your attention to briefly be with all the sensations happening in your body can also enhance a pleasant perceptual experience, such as a sunset or your favorite musicians in concert. It grounds you in the experience of yourself as well as what your senses are experiencing.

The power you gain through powerthinking methods is not only the ability to recognize your mode of thinking (right brain/left brain or VAK), but also the ability to deliberately shift your mode to match the learning task, the desired state, or the social situation at hand. This is the tool to balance thinking and feeling.

PART THREE

MEMORY
STATES

CHAPTER SIX

How to improve

your memory

I'll never forget what's his name.
—NORMAN PLISCOU

The famous memory expert Harry Loraine once memorized the first three hundred pages of the Manhattan telephone directory—over thirty thousand names and numbers.[1] He believes that developing a good memory is easy. It is like developing any other skill, such as driving a car or learning to use a computer.

Memory performs the remarkable function of connecting the past with the present. Without it we would wake up each morning not knowing our name, how to speak, how to make breakfast, or how to get dressed. When people claim to have poor memories, they are focusing on the small fraction of facts they temporarily cannot recall, as opposed to the enormous majority of life they do remember.

Memory is our constant companion[2]—our tutor, our library, the poet with whom we all travel. It allows life to become simpler from birth through adulthood as we learn from experience and are better able to act more efficiently in new situations. Furthermore, memory is the basis of analytical reasoning, decision making, and problem solving.

HOW MEMORY WORKS

Donny had just gotten up enough courage at the party to introduce himself to Carla and strike up a conversation. They hit it off well, and he asked for her phone number as she was leaving. Neither of them had anything to write with, so he decided to impress her by memorizing the number after hearing it just once.

As she left he knew he had about fifteen seconds to find a paper and pencil to write it down. He pictured the numbers, made a few associations with them, and tested himself over graduated intervals to encode the number effectively into his long-term memory. A few days later, when he phoned her, he still knew her number by heart.

This illustrates the "three r's" of memory—*reception* of the information into short-term memory, *registration* or *encoding* the material into long-term memory, and *recalling* it back out of long-term memory. The first two processes take place automatically, but recall depends on the quality of encoding. The more associations you make with the material, the easier it is to recall. The secret of memory training is to transfer the material as quickly as possible from short-term to long-term memory with encoding that makes it easy to access. Forgetful people have recall problems, not memory problems.

No one knows the exact mechanics of how memory is created and stored, but we do know some of the details. Short-term memory, which gives you enough time to get a telephone number from directory assistance and dial the number, lasts up to about fifteen seconds. Short-term memory seems to be related to electrical activity in the brain, where electrical impulses travel from neuron to neuron along axons and dendrites. Memory formation involves creation of neuro-transmiters, which in turn facilitate the passage of electrical impulses. The electrical signals and neurotransmitters somehow change the neurons, leaving behind a "memory trace"—probably through the formation of certain proteins.

Long-term memory—such as remembering your name, how to tie your shoes, and your personal history—usually lasts a lifetime, although recall may become more problematic with age. Interestingly, a relatively recent study[3] shows that short-term memory seems to be more effective earlier in the day, while long-term memory seems to work better later in the day.

The brain's memory center seems to be an S-shaped ridge in the hippocampus, with some memory stored in the cerebral cortex. As discussed in Chapter Three, memory of auditory words and verbal detail is more associated with left-brain functioning, while memory of pictures, images, spatial relationships, and emotions is more associated with the right. Beyond that, we can categorize memory into seven types:[4]

1. *Unconscious processes*—remembering how to breathe, how to digest food, and instinctual memory.
2. *Sensual memory*—remembering the feeling of a warm bath or how a strawberry tastes.
3. *Skills*—remembering how to swim, how to write, how to walk.
4. *Language*—remembering the meanings of all the words and phrases you commonly use.
5. *Facts*—remembering the number of feet in a mile, how to spell, how to balance your checkbook.
6. *Past events*—remembering the first time you fell in love or last year's birthday party.
7. *Future plans*—wanting to remember to get a birthday present for your friend or to put out the garbage for tomorrow morning's pickup.

Each type of memory except item 1 can involve visual, auditory, and kinesthetic recall, and almost everybody has nearly a perfect memory for items 1 through 4. What usually concerns us is items five through 7, and even here, the problem is effective encoding and recall, as opposed to memory.

As children most of us learned basic factual material by "over-learning"—endless repetition of our address, "ABC's," multiplication tables, etc. As we become older such brute-force tactics became tedious, boring, and exhausting. The bad news is that many of us were left with a negative association or *anchor* that memorizing is not fun. The good news is that there are much easier and more effective ways to remember. In fact, mere repetition may have a dulling, hypnotic effect and may not enhance memory, as Exercise 15 illustrates.

EXERCISE 15

Right now, without looking, describe and roughly sketch the back of a dime. You probably handle dimes thousands of times per year. Speak out or jot down whatever features you can remember.

If you don't remember much detail, don't be alarmed. You are probably in the majority.

I wonder how many times you have had an experience like this: You are working on a project when you get distracted and look over at a newspaper. The article is about an increase in the price of gasoline, so you think about the Middle East. That reminds you of Africa, at which point you think of the drought in Ethiopia, and your thought turns to food. Now you start to feel hungry, when suddenly it occurs to you that you were supposed to meet your friend at a restaurant five minutes ago, so off you go. The association of one idea with another is the basic mechanics of effective encoding and recall.

Trying to recall one unconnected memory among millions of others would be like walking into a library and finding the books arranged at random with no numbering system. The more organized the numbering system, the easier it will be to find a book. In a similar way, the more visual, auditory, and kinesthetic associations we use to encode new knowledge, the easier it will be to access the memory. The overlearning we endured as children may have been necessary to some extent because we didn't have as much prior knowledge to associate with new information.

EXERCISE 16

Start with the first line, with a sequence of five shapes. Glance at it for up to four seconds and then write down the sequence on a piece of paper without looking back. After you finish, check your results.

Now go on to the next line, with a sequence of six shapes. Again glance at it for up to four seconds and write down the sequence without looking back. Once you've reconstructed it, again check your results. Continue with the longer sequences.

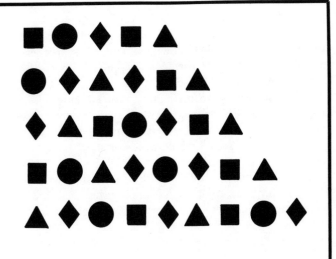

FIGURE 6.1

Most people find it increasingly difficult to remember the sequence as they get to seven or more shapes.

THE MAGIC NUMBER SEVEN

George Miller[5] of Harvard University discovered that the average person can retain up to about seven items in short-term memory—seven new names at a party, seven numbers, seven items on a grocery list.

Miller discovered further that each of the seven units could consist of several items, and this would expand the number of items we can remember. As an example, we commonly break telephone numbers down into groups or "chunks"—for example, 1–408–967–3359, and perhaps another 3157 as a credit card number.

The process of breaking down a larger number of items into smaller chunks is called "downchunking." As another example, most of use probably learned Mississippi as Miss-iss-ippi, and the ABC's as ABCD—EFG—HIJK . . .

A reverse process to this, called "upchunking," is seeing the larger picture. Children with reading disorders are often still sounding out words one letter at a time, as they did in the first grade, instead of seeing whole words or short phrases as a single unit.

Downchunking, or breaking the material down into smaller units, is probably more a left-brain process. Upchunking, or seeing the bigger picture, is more likely a right-brain process.

A few additional features of memory are important to understand.

EXERCISE 17

Read through the following list of words at your normal pace without going back over any of them.

1. spoon
2. and
3. bread
4. squirrel
5. napkin
6. candy
7. when
8. dog
9. plate
10. there
11. salt
12. bird
13. cup
14. of
15. coffee
16. frog
17. King Kong
18. over
19. carrot
20. knife

Now, from memory, write down as many words as you can remember.

As you compare the words you remembered, you may notice several things about them. First, you may have remembered more words from the beginning. This is called the *primacy effect*—we tend to remember more from the first part of a class, a study session, or people we meet at a party.

You may have remembered more words from the end. This is called the *regency effect*, wherein memory is enhanced toward the end of the time period. You remember more from the end of a class period, what you've just read, or the last few items on a grocery list. These two effects together give a memory curve that looks like that shown in Figure 6.2.

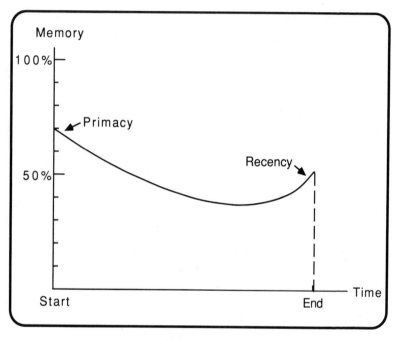

FIGURE 6.2

Another point is that you probably remembered "King Kong," because it stood out from the rest of the words. This principle, the *Von Restorff Effect*, is that unusual, colorful, or humorous items are easier to remember. What is even more interesting is that you probably remembered the words just before and just after "King Kong." Unusual words tend to "highlight" the words around them. This modifies the memory curve to look like that shown in Figure 6.3.

One last observation is that you may have grouped the words into the categories in which they fall—foodware, animals, food, and abstract words. Even though the words were not presented in groups, our unconscious looks for patterns and ways to organize things. As we'll see later, organizing by itself is a powerful memory tool.

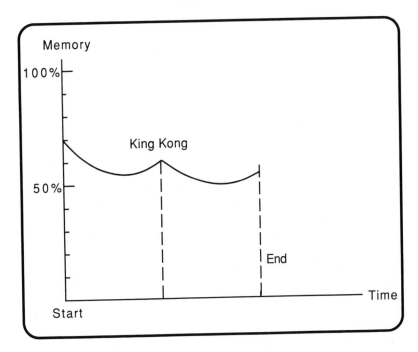

FIGURE 6.3

THE HISTORY OF MEMORY

One of the oldest systematic methods of memory began twenty-five hundred years ago, when Simonides of Ceos delivered a poorly received lyrical poem to an audience. Shortly after he left the room, the roof collapsed, killing many of the guests. Simonides was asked to help identify the guests, many of whom were no longer recognizable. By recalling where each guest was sitting, he was able to identify them.

From this tragedy Cicero developed one of the first systems of *mnemonics* (pronounced neh-mon-iks)—associating items to be remembered with places in a room. This system was useful in the ancient world, where not all knowledge was written. Roman orators later adapted this system to deliver speeches by the system of loci—associating each part of a speech with a place in their home. To deliver a speech they would mentally take a walk around their home, and each location would remind them of that part of the speech. This practice is still reflected in our language by the phrases "in the first place," "in the second place," etc.

St. Thomas Aquinas in the thirteenth century revived some of Aristotle's ideas on memory and formulated laws of remembering, a few of which connect with the modern neurolinguistic programming concept of *memory anchors*. St. Thomas observed that one memory evokes another if they are similar, if they are opposite, or if they occur simultaneously. Also, the more vivid the association, the easier it is to remember.

The father of modern experimental memory research was Hermann Ebbinghaus, who conducted experiments in Germany from 1879 to 1885. He knew the strong effects of association and meaning on memory, so he eliminated these factors in his research by trying to remember long lists of nonsense syllables like wux, zop, trefth, etc.

He soon discovered a law of forgetting—that after learning these lists, forgetting was highest just after learning the words, and gradually decreased with time. On average, 50 percent of the words were forgotten within one hour, 60 percent within nine hours, and 80 percent within a month.[6] Recall of the words can be graphed as shown in Figure 6.4.

Research since Ebbinghaus has confirmed the shape of his forgetting curve, with two qualifications: (1) The greater the meaning and the interest level, the slower the rate of forgetting, and (2) the reminiscent effect: For a few minutes to ten minutes after a class or study session, recall increases as we unconsciously integrate the material. These two qualifications modify the curve shown in Figure 6.5.

By taking the opposite approach as Ebbinghaus and including association, organization, meaning, and interest, we can greatly reduce the rate of forgetting.

WHY WE FORGET
- -

Have you ever begun to introduce two friends and forgotten one of their names? Or maybe you left your keys in a "safe" place, only to find they've disappeared when you go to find them. Memory lapses, a common annoyance for many of us when we are younger, can become terrifying as we get older.

On the other hand, remembering small, seemingly insignificant

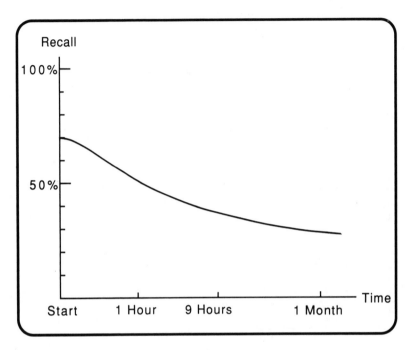

FIGURE 6.4

details about someone can be regarded as flattery. I remember walking into Ronnie's Shoe Store in San Jose, California, to buy a new pair of shoes. The owner struck up a conversation and seemed genuinely interested in learning about me. A year later, when I walked into the same store, the owner immediately said, "Oh, aren't you the physics professor over at West Valley College?" As you can imagine, I've bought all my shoes from him ever since.

Forgetfulness can happen in four ways:

1. We draw a complete blank.
2. The information is "on the tip of our tongue," and we feel frustrated with not being able to access it.
3. Recall is incomplete.
4. Wires get crossed, and we "remember" what's not so.

Again, it's doubtful that we actually forget, but why we have difficulty recalling is not completely known. Seven factors may contribute:

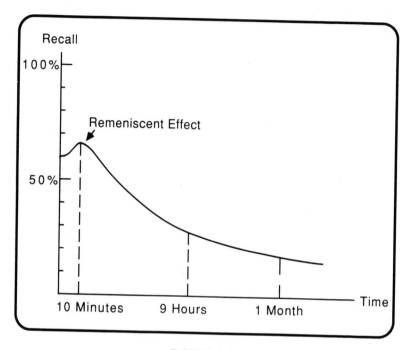

FIGURE 6.5

1. *Memory "traces"* may fade with time. Perhaps the cellular protein changes that took place to store memory revert back to their original state, like house paint eventually fading with exposure to sunlight. This once-popular theory has been widely replaced with the "interference theory."
2. *Interference*—as we accumulate more memories, the brain has increasing difficulty distinguishing among them, especially memories with similar associations or meaning. The problem is not so much one of overcrowding as of not having a specific enough retrieval system.
3. *Negative thinking* based on self-talk such as "I have such poor memory," "I can never remember anything," or "I must be getting old because my memory's shot" can help program the brain to bring about these self-fulfilling prophesies.
4. *Absentmindedness* happens when we don't think about what we're doing and function on "automatic pilot." Poor encoding results by not paying attention, thinking the information is not important, or not understanding it in the first place.

5. *Freud's repressive forgetting* occurs when certain memories are painful, threatening to the individual, or conflict with a person's values or beliefs.

6. *Smoking* decreases blood oxygen and adds significant amounts of carbon monoxide to the circulatory system, with adverse effects on the heart, lungs, psychomotor functioning, and memory. In one study,[7] smokers experienced a 24 percent reduction in memory after just one cigarette.

7. *Alcohol* and other drugs measurably impair memory.[8]

A pertinent question related to forgetting is: How much do we really want to remember? One estimate[9] is that we can recall about one of every hundred bits of information we encounter in daily life. The famous Spanish writer Jorge Luis Borges tells the story[10] of a boy who fell off of a horse and suddenly could remember literally everything that happened to him—the shape of each leaf on every tree he passed, each word in every conversation with each person he encountered. Life became like viewing a color print too close and seeing the individual dots instead of the whole picture; he became an idiot.

Perhaps some memory loss with age is more a matter of unconscious wisdom in choosing to remember only what's important. This may be valuable as long as we have the *choice* to forget what we want and can just as easily remember.

SIX TIPS FOR A SHARPER MEMORY

Since most of us have cultivated the ability to forget, how can we better develop the choice to remember? For especially difficult memory material such as Japanese vocabulary words or the names of bones and muscles, the supermemory techniques presented in Chapter Eight constitute the most effective approach. In this section we will explore six powerful strategies to improve memory in general. In Chapter Seven we will focus specifically on techniques to improve visual, auditory, and kinesthetic recall.

1. *Set up a state conducive to memory.* A restful, relaxed state with your physiology is useful to improve memory. For your IR's, motivation and interest are the strongest driving forces to

improve memory. If you are not motivated or interested in what you want to remember, imagine what it would be like if you were. How would you feel? How would things sound? How would they
look?

2. *Make memory sensory.* Were you to learn the rare English word *mackel*, meaning "a blurred print," you could tie in the information with your senses in one of three ways.

- *Visual imagery.* You might notice that mackel sounds a bit like mackerel, so you might imagine (V^i) a mackerel jumping up and down on a piece of paper, blurring the print. Thus you could remember "mackel—a blurred print" using that internal visual image.
- *Auditory imagery.* You might speak the word and its definition aloud (A^e) and then imagine yourself speaking it aloud (A^i). You might speak it, whisper it, and subvocalize it a couple of times. Either approach establishes an auditory recall.
- *Kinesthetic Imagery.* You might write the word and its definition (K^e), and then imagine yourself writing it (K^i). Get one of those four-colored pens and print the definition in capital letters, switch colors and print it in small letters, switch again and write it in script. Writing something in upper case, lower case, and script a few times produces imagery that is both kinesthetic and visual. If you speak as you write the definition, you add the auditory and thus cover the senses.

From my personal experience, kinesthetic imagery is most useful in technical fields such as mathematics, computer programming, and accounting. As a graduate student in physics, I had long equations with complicated derivations to memorize. I was not familiar with sensory memory techniques, but I discovered that if I simply wrote out the material a few times, I had it memorized. I find that most people attending my seminars instinctively do the same.

Another approach to make memory more kinesthetic is to connect it with feelings and emotions. People who remember the day John F. Kennedy was assassinated have never forgotten the fine details of what they were doing that day. If you think of a day that was especially traumatic—the death of a close friend or relative—or a day that was an emotional high point for you, you probably have a similar experience with unusual recall of details. Connecting memory with emotions relates to the NLP concept of anchors we'll be discussing later.

3. *Use graduated interval recall.* This is a powerful strategy to encode memory from short-term to long-term painlessly. Although the general strategy has been known for some time, the Sybervision® Corporation has recently popularized contributions made to this method by Dr. Paul Pimsleur, who applied the method to foreign-language acquisition.[11]

Dr. Pimsleur realized that the pure-repetition method of most foreign-language courses has a dulling, hypnotic effect and is not particularly effective. A powerful alternative is to ask the learner to reproduce a word or phrase at certain time intervals. The timing is crucial. If the interval between learning and being tested is too short or too long, the encoding loses effectiveness.

After learning new material, the learner is immediately tested. After a certain time interval, the learner is retested. Subsequent intervals become longer, allowing a smooth transition from short to stable long-term memory.

Sybervision® and Powerlearning® Systems have each structured foreign-language courses using this principle. Sybervision® claims that nine of ten people using this method can acquire a 1 + level of fluency* practicing one-half hour per day for only thirty days. I have personally experienced this and can verify the claims are true.

If you were learning Japanese words, technical definitions, or names at a party, you might proceed like this:

- Repeat the word or definition as you learn it.
- Test yourself on it within about eight to twelve seconds (transfer short-term to long-term memory).
- Test yourself again within thirty to fifty seconds (optional).
- Test yourself again within ninety seconds to three minutes (optional).

*Conversationally "intermediate high" as established by the FSI (U.S. government's Foreign Service Institute).

- Test yourself again within five to ten minutes.
- At this point you should have secured a good encoding for long-term memory. A few more reviews following a pattern given in Chapter Ten will further stabilize your long-term memory.

This pattern is particularly useful for auditory information such as foreign words or people's names. Of all the senses, auditory is the most difficult for most people to remember. This pattern is also an ideal structure for audio cassette tapes you can listen to while commuting. As you practice, you may require fewer repetitions than the pattern, and you can follow the timing guidelines in a general way that works for you.

EXERCISE 18

What are the two missing letters in the following sequence? J I H G F E _ _ B A. Of course, it's easy to recognize the alphabet backward and the missing "D" and "C."

See if you can identify the missing letters in Figure 6.6.

This pattern is not so obvious, so if you haven't already done so, read the letters as in Figure 6.7

You can now easily identify each missing letter as a "Y" and can memorize the exact sequence immediately. If you know the letters but not the pattern, it would take some brute-force memorizing to remember it. Even with that, you would probably forget the sequence as quickly as you memorized it.

---

1. *Look for principles and patterns of organization.* In one study at Stanford University,[12] two groups were each given 112 words to learn. One group was instructed to sort the words into four categories: occupations, animals, forms of transportation, and clothing items. The other group just learned the words at random. The sorters were able to learn two to three times more words than the random memorizers.

   In fact, other studies[13] have shown that organization by itself

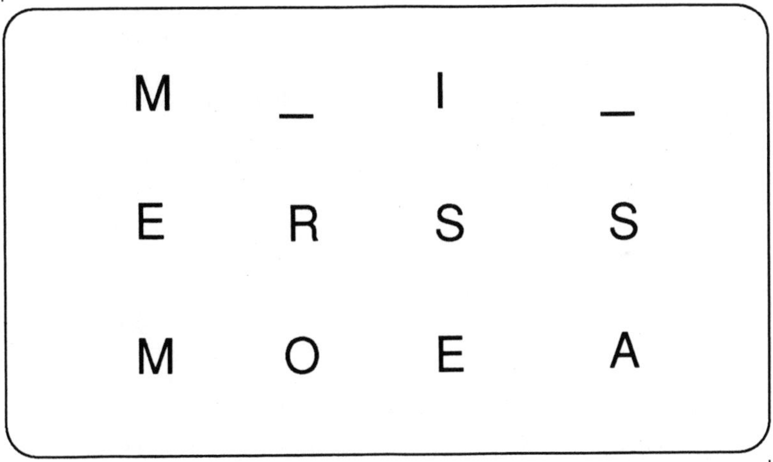

M   _   I   _

E   R   S   S

M   O   E   A

FIGURE 6.6

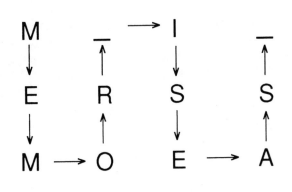

FIGURE 6.7

is just as effective as memorizing. George Korona[14] describes a study in which two groups were each given three minutes to learn a sequence of numbers. One group looked for principles while the other group just memorized. After three minutes the recall of each of the two groups was about the same. However, after three weeks none of the memorizers remembered the sequence, while 23 percent of the principle recognizers still remembered all the numbers.

Organizing material into meaningful patterns promotes active involvement and personal meaning, both of which enhance memory. This is one reason why note taking can be useful—particularly pattern discovery maps. This also explains the value of studying the grammatical structure of a foreign language.

2. *Future pace, a desired memory with a sensory stimulus.* The term *future pace*, used in NLP, is the process of projecting a desired behavior into future situations that might test that behavior. If you need to stop at the post office on the way to work, imagine the scenery you will naturally see as you approach the vicinity of the post office, and visualize yourself remembering to stop off. If the visual image of the scenery is anchored strongly enough with the feeling of remembering, seeing the scenery will automatically trigger the memory. Similarly, you might future-pace the sound of a friend's voice to remind you to ask if you can borrow her tennis racquet.

3. *Make memory a habit.* Good memory is a skill. The more you practice and trust the workings of your unconscious, along with avoiding negative self talk about your memory and having to rely on elaborate lists, the sharper your memory will become. These simple techniques should help memory become part of everyday life.

CHAPTER SEVEN

VISUAL, AUDITORY, AND KINESTHETIC MEMORY

It's not so astonishing the number of things I can't remember, as the number of things I can remember that aren't so.

—MARK TWAIN

Artists and photographers often have extraordinary recall of visual detail. Composers and expert debaters can usually remember fine nuances of sound and words most of us would find insignificant, while athletes and dancers are superb with remembering psychomotor skills and movement. In this chapter we will focus on developing specific skills to access visual, auditory, and kinesthetic memories.

ENHANCING YOUR VISUAL RECALL

Most people have a much better visual memory than they think. The ability to close the eyes and see vivid detail in sharp focus and color is quite rare. Instead, most of us see more vague images, with just enough general structure and form to allow us to act and make decisions. One study[1] on five hundred people showed that 97 percent of them had some visual imagery, even if vague; 92 percent also had auditory imagery—they could imagine words or sounds.

105

Ralph N. Haber[2] of the University of Rochester showed subjects twenty-five hundred pictures during seven hours spread over three days. They saw a new picture every ten seconds. After viewing all the slides, they saw three hundred pairs of pictures—one they had seen and another, similar picture they hadn't seen. At that point they were asked to identify the picture they had seen. In some cases they were given a reversed, mirror image of the one they had seen.

The results were that the subjects averaged 85 to 90 percent correct. In fact, even when the study was repeated and viewing the photos was speeded up ten times, the scores were still high. The evidence in this and other studies indicates that visual recall is nearly perfect for most of us.

In another study[3] it was found that we can all improve memory by using visual imagery. People with vague, indistinct images were able to improve memory to 70 percent when given instruction to visualize what they were to remember. People with sharp, clear visual images were able to improve to 95 percent. What is fascinating is that each group had about the same *change* or *increase*. Of course, if we can learn to improve the clarity of what we visualize, our memory will improve. Here are some ways to sharpen your visual memory:

1. *Carefully observe an object*. Pick one object each day—preferably something interesting or amusing—and spend a few minutes studying it. Later in the day, recall as many details about the object as you can. Then compare your memory with the object to see how you did. With a little practice you'll be surprised how your visual recall improves.
2. *Assume visual recall training*.
   - visual posture (upright), breathing (shallow and high in the chest), and your eye position.
   - sensory overlap
   - spontaneous visualization

REMEMBERING WHAT YOU'VE HEARD

"What do you mean, where is dinner? You promised to take me out tonight," snapped Don. "I didn't say that. You promised me you'd make lasagne for us," retorted Doris.

Most of our interpersonal communication and classroom learning involve the auditory mode, yet of the three types of memory—visual, auditory, and kinesthetic—most of us find auditory to be the least reliable. The problem has two parts: recalling what you heard, and listening carefully in the first place.

When listening to a conversation or a lecture, there are six ways to improve your listening skills and thus the likelihood of remembering what you heard.[4]

1. *W.I.I.F.M?* Think, "What's in it for me?" If you are clearly aware of how you might benefit from listening, you are more than halfway toward setting up an appropriate state.

2. *Notice the mode of delivery but only judge the content.* It has been estimated that only 7 percent of the message in conversation is communicated with words,[5] 38 percent of the message lies in voice inflections and perceived attitudes about the person, and 55 percent is based on nonverbal body language. That is why we are often more affected by how someone says something vs. what they actually said.

3. *Distractions.* When you become aware of being distracted from what the person is saying, easily and gently bring your attention back. Getting upset with yourself or the outside distraction only compounds the interruption.

4. *Pay attention to your physiology.* Careful listening is work. Periodic stretching, walking, and breaks help maintain long-term focus.

5. *For boring or hard-to-follow speakers.* Take the viewpoint of a strongly opposed critic. Expert debaters have learned to listen carefully for holes in the opponent's argument and points to refute. You might also imagine that you were going to write a critique of the talk. How would you be listening to write a convincing article taking the opposite viewpoint of the speaker?

6. *Assume auditory recall training.*
   - eyes in your direction (toward one side)
   - listening longer
   - generalized and focused listening
   - mirroring unconscious mannerisms
   - sensory overlap in purely auditory situations (e.g., the telephone)

To recall what you've heard after listening, use pattern discovery maps during a lecture or after a conversation to construct a picture of what was said and to engage a more whole-brain approach to memory. By incorporating these methods to improve your listening and hearing skills, you will find your sensory experience of life richer. Also, it will be less likely that information will go "in one ear and out the other."

KINESTHETIC RECALL AND MEMORY ANCHORS

Kinesthetic memory, like visual memory, is nearly perfect for most people. If you haven't ridden a bicycle or gone swimming for five years, you probably won't have to start over to relearn these skills. Of course, remembering the subtleties of finely tuned psychomotor skills, such as controlling your ace serve in tennis, is the subject of peak-performance research in athletics and dance.

You can enhance kinesthetic recall in a couple of ways:

1. *Assume kinesthetic recall training.*

   • a relaxed posture
   • deep diaphragm breathing
   • looking down

2. *Use memory anchors.* This is a nice way to take advantage of the kinesthetic component of memory. A *memory anchor* occurs when we have an intense emotional or tactile kinesthetic experience and something else happens coincidentally. The unconscious then links them together in the future.

   Have you ever walked into a department store and smelled a perfume you haven't smelled in ten years? You feel yourself pulled back in time. Or maybe you are driving down the highway listening to the radio. A song comes on that was popular when you were in high school, and suddenly you are back on a date in your junior year. The stimulus of the smell or the music was enough to "fire" the anchor—to elicit feelings, sights, or sounds connected or anchored to the stimulus.

   A bizarre example of a memory anchor was illustrated with scuba divers[5] in a study done by Drs. Alan D. Baddeley and

Duncan R. Godden. The divers were given forty unrelated words to remember while they were under water. Half of the group was tested on the words out of the water, while the other half was tested under water. The ones tested under water remembered twice as many words as the dry testers.

This and many other studies suggest that our mood and the environment become anchored to what we are learning. Thus, re-creating the mood and the environment can help facilitate recall. Certainly happy occurrences evoke happy memories, and a depressed state evokes depressing memories. Likewise, if you can study and succeed answering questions in the same room you will be tested in, this can facilitate recall when you are tested.

Memory anchors have influenced pioneers in accelerated learning methods like Dr. Donald Schuster of Iowa State University in Ames to beautify their learning environment with plants, posters, subliminal messages, stately music, and color—partly to engage the right brain in the learning process better and partly to anchor learning to that beauty.

Many students incur too much stress during last-minute study for a test. Then when they take the test, they experience the same tension and stress. And guess what? It works. The stimulus of the stress fires the anchor of the memory. On the other hand, people using super memory techniques in Chapter Eight learn the material in a relaxed, nurturing, playful environment. Taking the test in that same environment again fires the memory anchor. Now think about it. Which way would you rather learn?

In his research Dr. Schuster has discovered that someone who is used to stressful learning may initially not do as well when taught stress-free learning. After some practice, however, this learning becomes more effective than the old way.

DISCOVERING YOUR MAGIC KEY FOR MEMORY

One of the most powerful ways to engage your senses to improve memory is to discover your personal key or formula for remembering. This is the specific sequence of internal and external visual, auditory, and kinesthetic images you already use when you're most successful at remembering.

EXERCISE 19: YOUR MEMORY AND LEARNING KEY

1. To begin, think of a specific time in the past when you remembered something especially well. Mentally put yourself back in that situation. It is crucial you engage as much of that experience as possible as if it were *happening now*.

2. What is the first thing necessary for you to have a strong memory? Did you need to *see* what you wanted to remember (visual external: V^e), or *hear* someone tell you about it (auditory external: A^e), or move with it, get a *feeling* for it, or write it down (kinesthetic external: K^e)? Again, focus on that very *first* thing that had to happen. Chances are it will be the same as your primary modality discovered in the internal representation assessment test.

3. Once you have seen, heard, or felt what you want to remember, what happens inside? Do you picture or visualize it (visual internal: V^i), or hear an internal voice repeating it inside (auditory internal: A^i), or perhaps get a sense or feeling of what you want to remember, or feel it in your body (kinesthetic internal: K^i)?

4. What happens next? Do you need to see it again, hear more about, explain it to someone, or do it (V^e, A^e, or K^e)? Or do you further process it internally with pictures, sounds, or feelings (V^i, A^i, or K^i)?

5. There may be additional steps involving internal or external processing, although the whole sequence typically involves only two to four steps.

6. The last step is when you *know* that you remember it correctly. How do you *know* that you know it? Quite often this is an internal sense or feeling (K^i), although it could also be an internal auditory or visual comparison (A^i or V^i).

7. Once you have listed the steps, you might construct a pattern discovery map with the information. To complete and refine your key, add submodalities that enhance various steps.

The exact sequence of steps in this key is like a recipe. If you do the steps in the proper order, you get the results. If you reverse any of the steps, it doesn't work.

As an example, my key to understand and remember physics is first to read it V^e and try to sense how it works K^i. I then write and problem-solve with it K^e. I try to see the whole picture V^i, and finally know that I understand it K^i. Sometimes I add a step just before the last of explaining it to someone else (A^e), since my formula doesn't otherwise have an auditory component. Thus my key is as in Figure 7.1.

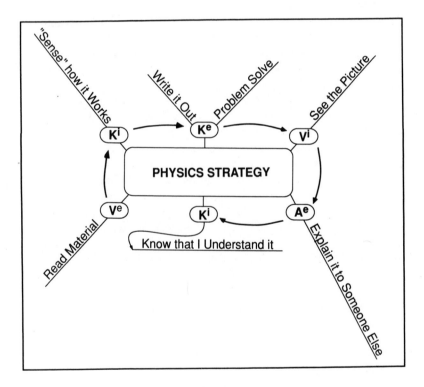

FIGURE 7.1

A NEW APPROACH TO MNEMONICS

When we read books on memory, we find instructions to create associations, visualizations, and other *mnemonic* devices to aid memory. The word *mnemonic* means an associative device designed to aid memory. Examples of mnemonics may include:

- You meet a lady, Dana Crosby. To remember her name, you imagine a Great *Dane* with her face getting stung by a *cross bee.*
- You want to remember the rare English word *kidcote*, meaning jail. You might imagine Billy the *Kid* wearing a *coat* in jail.
- You're trying to remember the Portuguese word *noz* (pronounced nawsh), meaning walnut. You might imagine a walnut feeling nauseous.

Books on memory are consistent in telling us we should create associations for memory, but no one provides a systematic way to create these mnemonic connections. Some people who read memory books can naturally think of associations, but many of us find the process time-consuming, tedious, and not applicable to most of what we need to remember.

I ask my seminar participants, "If you had a systematic process to create mentally the kinds of images and associations we've talked about, how could you use that personally? Would it even be useful to you personally?" Participants respond that if they did have such a system, they could use it to remember

- names and faces
- historical dates
- vocabulary words
- foreign words
- shopping lists

A method I've developed strongly facilitates creation of these associations and uses pattern discovery maps. To illustrate how you might use a map to create a visual picture or mnemonic device, imagine you were studying technical terms or vocabulary words and you come across the rare English word *basiate*, which means "to kiss." Split the word into syllables, with each syllable being the center of a pattern discovery map. The entire meaning can also be a map center. The centers would then look as in Figure 7.2.

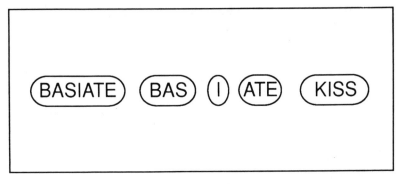

FIGURE 7.2

Now create three or four connections or associations from each syllable and the meaning. A connection can be

- a similar-sounding word
- a word you are reminded of
- another word that contains the syllable
- a rhymed word

For "bas" you might think of words such as fish, basket, bass, and shoes. For "I" you might think of me, eye, and aye. For "ate" you might be reminded of eat, food, the number 8, and the rhymed word mate. For the meaning "kiss" perhaps pucker, love, candy, and the rock band named Kiss. Adding these connections creates something like that shown in Figure 7.3.

It takes about a minute or two to do this process. But once you've gone through it, it is unlikely you'll forget the meaning. Instead of having just the words, you've now created a picture. Pictures are always easier to remember than words. However, something else may happen in the process. You might think of a story connecting basiate with kiss—connecting a few but not all of the associations.

For example, you might imagine a largemouth *bass* giving you a *kiss* just before you *ate* it. Or maybe I got a *bass* for *me* at *8*:00 P.M. so I could

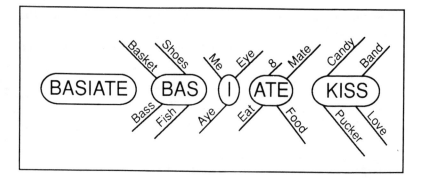

FIGURE 7.3

play with the *Kiss* band. Perhaps *I* took a candy *kiss* out of the *bas*ket and gave it to my m*ate*.

Look at all the possibilities for creating a story from the map, as opposed to just looking at the definition. The picture is sufficient and the story is not necessary, but creating the story makes the process more fun.

EXERCISE 20

Try this process out for yourself with the rare English word *kidcote*, meaning jail.

Sometimes when people first see this process, it seems like too much work just to connect the word with its meaning. In my seminars, I usually ask how many participants have ever taken tennis lessons. To those who respond, I ask if they remember the first day on the court: Ready position . . . pivot sideways on the balls of your feet . . . all right, racket head back, perpendicular to the ground . . . now swing low to high . . . remember to follow through . . . on and on. By the time you tried to do all that, the ball was likely back at the fence. It probably seemed awkward and mechanical. With practice, however, you began to flow properly through the movement without thinking about it. It's like that with this process.

Probably the only difference between you and a memory expert who can get onstage and name a hundred names and addresses of people in the audience is that the memory expert does something similar to the mapping process unconsciously and automatically. For you it is initially a mechanical process, but with time it gets easier, quicker, and more automatic.

In my experience studying foreign languages, I find that many Spanish, French, and German words are so similar to English that I don't have to do anything special to learn them. With other words, however, I couldn't begin to imagine how they connect with English. By using the mapping technique, I can always create a picture and often a story for each word. For a list of words I use a stack of 3″ by 5″ cards, with one map on each card.

This technique to create mnemonics systematically is the last of the memory secrets used unconsciously by the best visual, auditory, and kinesthetic learners. With practice we can begin to develop the seemingly elusive perceptual and memory skills of the artists, composers, athletes, and dancers we all admire.

CHAPTER EIGHT

SUPERMEMORY

Man's mind, stretched to a new idea, never goes back to its original dimension.
—OLIVER WENDELL HOLMES

Is it really possible to learn a foreign language in one month or to speed up learning three to ten times? This is what the authors of the popular book *Superlearning* claim. Can learning and memory be accelerated yet be stress-free? This chapter presents a practical introduction to super-memory techniques based on Superlearning®,* my training in these methods, and my years of experience training others to use them in my Powerlearning® seminars given throughout the United States.

BACKGROUND OF SUPERMEMORY METHODS

Six thousand years ago, before the advent of written language, techniques related to Superlearning® probably flourished. Supermemory may have been a tool of necessity—the only way to pass down

---

*Superlearning® is the registered trademark and service mark of Superlearning® Inc., 450 Seventh Avenue, New York, N.Y. 10123

folklore, legend, and practical knowledge for survival. The techniques were most likely rooted in music, chants, drama, rhythm, and emotion.

Even today some cultures, such as the Maoris in New Zealand,[1] display remarkable feats of memory. One leader, Chief Kau Matana, could reportedly recite the entire history of their tribe in three days without notes, and their history covers forty-five generations extending over a thousand years. In India, pundits routinely memorize their religious scriptures in case a catastrophe destroys all the books.

In the 1950s Dr. Georgi Lozanov,[2] a Bulgarian physician and psychologist, began a systematic study of those few people left today with the gift of extraordinary memory, concentration, and learning ability. His Ph.D. thesis was a study on the application of suggestion to medicine and education. Of special interest to him were people having hypermnesia or "photographic memory," as well as Indian yogis and pundits with remarkable mental skills.

He wondered if there were any patterns in how they learn and concentrate, or any systematic methods. In his research, he discovered certain patterns of rhythm, relaxation, music, and breathing that convinced him that we all can develop supermemory skills. Lozanov then combined his observations with his own ideas from psychotherapy to develop a system called *Suggestopedia*.

Two American adaptations of Suggestopedia are now popularly called SALT (Suggestive Accelerative Learning and Teaching) and Superlearning®. My approach to supermemory incorporates methods from these adaptations together with principles from NLP, pattern discovery maps, and keys.

In any case, Lozanov tested his new system with foreign languages and other types of education and training. The results were phenomenal. Reports began circulating of people learning a thousand foreign words in one day, becoming fluent in a foreign language within one month, and speeding up learning ten to fifty times.

Word of these techniques first reached the West through *Psychic Discoveries Behind the Iron Curtain** by Sheila Ostrander and Lynn Schroeder in 1970. Dr. Jane Bancroft, a professor at Scarborough College of the University of Toronto, was one of the first North American scholars to contact Lozanov and actually see firsthand what he was doing. Dr. Donald Schuster, a psychology professor at Iowa State University in Ames, read the initial account in *Psychic Discoveries*.

*(Englewood Cliffs: Prentice Hall, 1970)

With very little knowledge of the specifics of the methodology, Dr. Schuster, Ray Benitez Borden, and colleagues began experimenting with the principles and got encouraging results right from the start. This initial work eventually led to the formation of a professional society of educators and researchers using accelerated learning methods, The Society for Suggestive Accelerative Leaning and Teaching or SALT.* This group now has members throughout the world and publishes a quarterly research journal, as well as conducting annual conferences and teacher training courses.

In 1979 Ostrander and Schroeder published the book *Superlearning*®, an interpretation of Suggestopedia shared by the authors, Dr. Bancroft, and the SALT Society. Since its publication, *Superlearning*® has been a milestone in popularizing accelerated learning concepts.

HOW DO SUPERMEMORY METHODS WORK?
- -

The system I present in my seminars uses a unique combination of music, relaxation, suggestion, imagery, and play to promote accelerated, stress-free learning. This is accomplished by five key elements.

1. *A global approach to learning.* In various fields of study, including foreign languages, the strategy is a right-brain one of picking up broad general relationships before proceeding to finer detail. Pattern discovery maps can be useful toward this end.
2. *Rhythm.* With SALT and Superlearning®, you structure the material you want to commit to memory in a certain rhythm. You also accompany this with music of specific rhythm. You can even breathe in a similar rhythm. As yogis in India have known for centuries, certain rhythms make it easier to learn. This may correspond with natural internal biological rhythms.
3. *Suggestion.* Because Lozanov felt that suggestion is such a key component, he named his system "Suggestopedia." Suggestion is an integral part of how we communicate with others, and more importantly, how we communicate with ourselves through

*SALT Society, 3028 Emerson Avenue South, Minneapolis, MN 55408.

internal self-talk. We can inwardly reaffirm our confidence in ourselves as learners or call ourselves stupid and incapable. Positive inward suggestion can develop powerful links between the conscious and the unconscious, and allow for quick permanent changes in our skills and behavior.

Internally, you can tell yourself your tennis serves will be fast and accurate today, but it is more powerful to combine this message with the auditory submodalities that work best for you. This, together with *visualizing* the correct form and imagining how it *feels*, give power to your internal suggestions.

4. *Restful awareness.* Stress and anxiety often block memory. In contrast, a sufficiently deep state of relaxation can have the opposite effect of enhancing unconscious recall. Researchers have used instruments to monitor yogis when they perform remarkable physical and mental feats.[3] They found that the yogis' bodies are physically relaxed while their minds are intensely focused with a production of alpha waves. We call this state *restful awareness*.

Lozanov discovered that the Indian yogis with phenomenal memory can maintain restful awareness. They can stay in this state for extended periods of time. Supermemory methods take full advantage of this ancient knowledge and use a unique combination of rhythm, music, and breathing to maintain that state.

5. *Making work play.* Due to lack of confidence in our ability to learn and remember, many of us experience tension when we try to do these things. As a result, we strain our muscles, and then the physical and mental stresses actually reduce our memory and learning ability. A tired and frustrated learner may conclude that the material is beyond his or her ability—but often this isn't true.

Supermemory methods solve these problems through an approach called *infantilization*. We establish a childlike state for learning. As young children we were spontaneous, full of curiosity and questions, totally open to learning, and free of most of the learning blocks we have now. Even as adults we sometimes experience a childlike joy when we become so absorbed in work that it seems more like play. These times excite us, stretch us, challenge us, and make life richer.

Work is love made visible.
—Anonymous

Your six-step supermemory master key is shown in Figure 8.1.

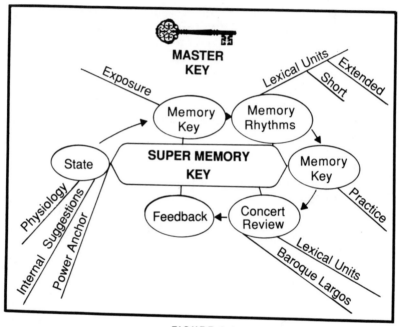

FIGURE 8.1

STEP ONE: STATE

This is a five- to six-minute phase designed to put you into an empowering state for learning, so as you can imagine we start with:

1. *Physiology.* In my seminars we begin with a minute or two of stretching. I select four or five from the group of simple exercises shown in Figures 8.2a and 8.2b. Hold each for seven to ten seconds.

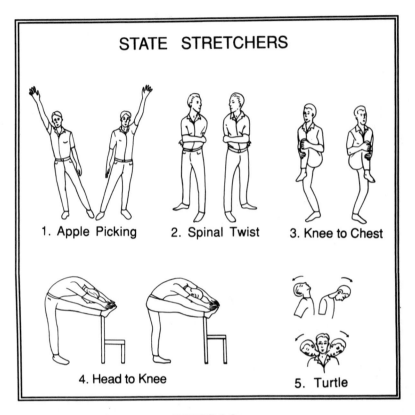

STATE STRETCHERS

1. Apple Picking   2. Spinal Twist   3. Knee to Chest

4. Head to Knee   5. Turtle

FIGURE 8.2a

To relax your physiology further you can spend a couple of minutes with *progressive relaxation*. Relax one muscle group at a time until your whole body feels relaxed and limp. Start from your head and work downward toward your feet. As an alternative, you can tense each muscle group and then relax it. After completing, slowly take five deep breaths, and as you exhale, feel your body going limp and melting into your chair.

An alternative for a relaxed state is called *Zen breathing*. Just observe your breathing for a few minutes without trying to control it. Whenever you breathe in, silently think "in" to yourself. When you breathe out, think "out." When you find your attention wandering, easily bring it back. Again, just observe your breathing for a few minutes without controlling.

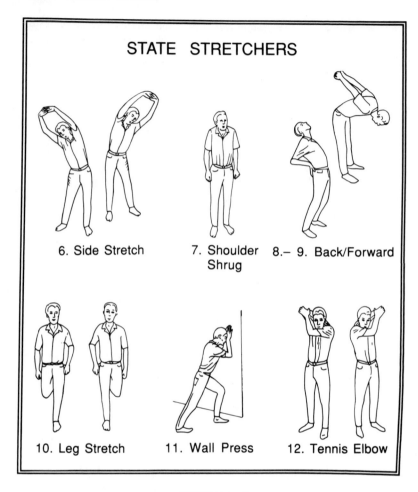

STATE STRETCHERS

6. Side Stretch

7. Shoulder Shrug

8.– 9. Back/Forward

10. Leg Stretch

11. Wall Press

12. Tennis Elbow

FIGURE 8.2b

Beyond this, just imagine how your body would feel if you were really excited about what you want to learn and remember. How would you be sitting? What posture would you assume? Would you be smiling with confidence? If you are not particularly excited about what you have to learn and remember, just imagine what it would be like if you were.

2. *Internal suggestions* provide a way to improve your IR's, that is, the quality of how you represent the learning task internally. Mentally project yourself into the activity. For example, if you

VISUALIZE

SEE MYSELF

are going to take a test, imagine yourself feeling confident and energetic. The adrenaline is starting to flow, and this leads you to peak performance. You are answering the questions, remembering everything, and working quickly.

When test-taking is this easy, notice what emotions you feel. What do you feel in your body? How do things look? How do they sound? Be sure to cover the modalities (VAK) and submodalities (close up or far away; bright or dim; soothing, inflected, or resonant voice; warm, light, or tingly feelings, etc.) that are most important for you. You might also thank yourself internally, as if you had already succeeded.

The other possibility for internal suggestions is to go back in time to a pleasant learning experience from the past. Maybe you had a hobby you were very good with. Or maybe there was a book that absorbed your interest so much you could hardly put it down. Think of some situation where you learned well and had fun learning. What emotions did you feel? How did your body feel? How did things look? How did they sound?

TRY A CLUSTER SEARCH

Consider the possibility of whatever you experienced in the past being available in the present for what you want to learn now. For example, if I could learn computer assembly language and have as much fun as I did learning how to ski, it would still be a lot of work. But if I'm having fun while I'm learning, it won't seem like work. Also, I will be much more effective at learning and remembering the material. Finally, thank your unconscious for allowing those feelings from the past to come into what you are doing now.

An easy way to get started with relaxation and internal suggestions is to purchase a prerecorded audiocassette tape. Powerlearning® Systems* offers a tape called *Learning Power*. Side 2 has five selections—each is a combination of relaxation and internal suggestions, and each lasts four to five minutes. Of course, once you get used to the process, you will probably want to put the exercises into your own words. That establishes more direct communication between you and your unconscious self.

How to Buy?

3. *Power Anchor.* This optional third step is one of the quickest

---

*Powerlearning® Systems, P.O. Box 496, Santa Cruz, CA 95061.

ways to establish an empowering state of motivation and high energy. Specifics of how to set up and fire a power anchor are discussed in Chapter Twelve. Once you have read that chapter and established a power anchor for yourself, it will only take a few seconds to engage that anchor.

STATE (FIVE TO SIX MINUTES)

1. Take a minute or two to stretch, using four or five of the exercises shown.
2. Relax yourself with a couple of minutes of

   • Progressive relaxation of one muscle group at a time; or
   • Zen breathing—just observing your breathing.

3. Imagine your posture and physical sensations if you were excited about what you want to learn and remember.
4. Do a few minutes of internal suggestions. You can mentally project successful learning with the sights, sounds, and feelings you will experience paying attention to important submodalities. The other alternative is going back to a past successful learning experience and bringing sights, sounds, and feelings from the past to the present learning task.
5. As an optional last step, employ a power anchor described in Chapter Twelve.

MAKE A TAPE

STEP TWO: MEMORY KEY FOR EXPOSURE AND UNDERSTANDING

pg. 110

Approach what you want to learn and remember through the first part of your memory and learning key from Chapter Seven. Proceed just far enough to gain exposure and understanding of what you want to remember. Obviously it does no good trying to memorize something you don't understand.

For example, the first three steps in my physics key are read the material (V^e), sense how it works (K^i), and write it out (K^e). At this point if I still don't understand it, I might reread it or have someone explain it to me (A^e).

Knowing your memory and learning key is crucial. Knowledge of your personal key allows you to customize supermemory to the way that works best for you.

STEP 3: MEMORY RHYTHMS[4]

After going through the first several steps of your memory key for initial exposure and understanding, notice which items or concepts you find most difficult to remember. This next step will greatly facilitate memorizing those most difficult items by structuring them in a certain rhythm. You can do this with a friend, a prerecorded audiocassette tape, or perhaps make a tape as part of this process.

Memory Rhythms with a Friend—Short Lexical Units

An easy approach is to work with a friend. Suppose you want to memorize a list of short ideas such as foreign words, short foreign phrases, technical definitions, spelling words, bones, muscles, equations, computer commands, or historical dates. The friend speaks for four seconds, pauses four seconds, speaks four seconds, and pauses four seconds alternately. Each four seconds of material, called a *short lexical unit*, consists of one complete idea, such as:

- a foreign word, the English translation, and the foreign word again
- the English version of the short phrase (not more than four or five words) and the foreign version
- a technical term or vocabulary word with its definition
- a word and its spelling (not more than eight or nine letters long)
- a bone or muscle, what it connects to, and what it does
- an equation
- a computer command and what it does
- a historical date and what happened on that date

As long as you can speak the information in seven to nine words or less, it will normally fit comfortably into four seconds. For example, a list of Portuguese words might be structured like this:

Speak four seconds	Pause four seconds
"*noz*, walnut, *noz*"	. . . .
"*pai*, father, *pai*"	. . . .

A list of bones in the big toe might be set up like this:

Speak four seconds	Pause four seconds
"At the end of the toe is the distal phalanx."	. . . .
"The second bone in is the proximal phalanx."	. . . .
"The base of the toe is the metatarsal."	. . . .

Lines of a poem can be set up in the same way:

Speak four seconds	Pause four seconds
"Shall I compare thee to a summer's day?	. . . .
Thou art more lovely and more temperate:	. . . .
Rough wings do shake the darling buds of May,	. . . .
And summer's lease hath all too short a date:"*	. . . .

Memory Rhythms with a Friend—Extended Lexical Units

Suppose, on the other hand, you are memorizing more extended ideas that don't fit into four seconds. Maybe you are memorizing principles from accounting or chemistry, or perhaps the spelling words or foreign phrases are too long for four seconds. In this case use *extended lexical units*. Speak the point in a complete sentence for however long it takes, and then pause about four seconds. If the point is more than one sentence long, each sentence is a separate lexical unit. For example, to solve ax + b = c for x:

*William Shakespeare, Sonnet 18.

Speak	*Pause four seconds*
"Subtract the quantity 'b' from both sides of the equation"	. . . .
"This gives ax = c−b"	. . . .
"Now divide both sides of the equation by the quantity 'a'"	. . . .
"This gives x equals the quantity (b−c) divided by a"	. . . .

If you were memorizing lines in a play, each sentence could be an extended lexical unit:

Speak	*Pause four seconds*
PRINCE: "Why, what a pox have I to do with my hostess of the tavern?"	. . . .
FAL: "Well, thou hast called her to a reckoning many a time and oft."	. . . .
PRINCE: "Did I ever call thee to pay thy part?"	. . . .
FAL: "No, I'll give thee thy due, thou hast paid all there."*	. . . .

—USE MAPPING—

If you were reviewing Chapters 4, 5, and 6 for a test, you could list the main points in sentences. Of course, list only the points you find most difficult to remember. You can get the easier points with the simpler reading and study techniques presented later.

Now have your friend speak short or extended lexical units with a four-second pause between units. While he or she does this, you have a photocopy of the list in front of you. While your friend reads aloud, you read silently.

If your list has short lexical units, you can also breathe a certain way to enhance the process. As your friend speaks, hold your breath in. When he or she stops, breathe out and in. Then, just as your friend starts to speak again, hold your breath in, etc. It's very simple. When they are speaking, you hold your breath in. When they are not speaking, you breathe—first out and then back in. The breathing is

*William Shakespeare, *Henry IV*; Act I.

synchronized so you are taking in a new breath of air each time you hear a new lexical unit. It is also part of the overall memory rhythm.

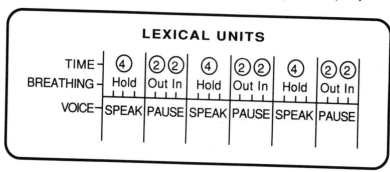

FIGURE 8.3

In my seminars some of the participants wonder why you have to do active organizing with a friend. Why couldn't you just speak the material yourself? The answer is that for short lexical units, you can't hold your breath and talk at the same time. If you have extended lexical units, you will not do this breathing pattern, but you may need the friend anyway for a later step.

Memory Rhythms on Your Own

Another approach if you want to use supermemory methods without a friend is to record an audiocassette tape. Once you have your list, speak the lexical unit into the tape recorder, pause four seconds, speak the next, pause four seconds again, etc. Once you've recorded on the tape, play it back, read along silently from your list, and do the breathing (for short units only). For extended units, just read along.

Of course, by the time you have (1) picked out the main points, (2) decided which of these are most difficult to remember, (3) set up your lexical units, and (4) recorded on your tape, you probably half-know the material already. You may want to stop after recording on the tape. If the material is not too difficult to remember, just recording on the tape is enough. If it is especially difficult, play back the tape, read silently, and do the breathing pattern if appropriate.

Appendix Four goes into detail on the mechanics of recording on your own tape with the appropriate timing.

STEP FOUR: MEMORY KEY
FOR PRACTICE

The supermemory strategy in this next step is to incorporate the rest of your memory key not covered in the second step. In most cases this requires some type of practice. For example, two of the remaining steps in my Physics key—problem-solving (K^e), and possibly explaining it to someone else (A^e)—are practice.

The practice could include the visual, auditory, and kinesthetic memory techniques or the mnemonic strategy. It might also involve creating pattern discovery maps to see broad general relationships.

SALT also encourages making such practice creative and innovative—making work into play. Thus if you are studying history, you might imagine yourself to be a magazine reporter. Suppose you could step into a time machine and travel back to that historical period. What questions would you ask those people? How do you think they would respond? How would you feel? How would you write your article?

Again, the idea here is that since you have to do some kind of practice to get the material down, why not make the practice creative, fun, and enjoyable? This not only makes the material easier to remember and the learning more effective but also reinforces the notion that learning can be fun.

STEP FIVE: THE CONCERT REVIEW

The concert review is probably what SALT and Superlearning® are best known for—the unique combination of music, breathing, and rhythm that promotes a relaxed state of restful awareness. In this stage you are committing the material you have set up in lexical units to a deeper level of memory.

At this point you need a friend or a prerecorded tape. The voice speaks a lexical until, pauses four seconds, speaks another unit, and pauses as before. Set up a comfortable and pleasant environment for yourself. Perhaps take your shoes off, sit in a comfortable, overstuffed chair, prop your feet up, close your eyes, and relax.

For extended lexical units, breathe normally. For short units, do the breathing pattern we discussed earlier. When the voice is speaking, hold your breath in. When the voice stops, breathe out and back in. When the voice speaks again, hold your breath in again, etc.

The procedure here is the same as in the memory rhythms step, but instead of reading along with the material, close your eyes and relax completely. In addition, the concert review uses music.

The use of music to accelerate learning dates back to antiquity. Oral tradition was often passed down in songs, chants, or verse. Even today the melody of a song enhances memorization of lyrics. In ancient Greece[5] people attended performances of the *Iliad* accompanied by the lute. Many reportedly walked away with the verses memorized.

For best results Lozanov recommended baroque largos at about sixty beats per minute. Baroque dates from the late Renaissance to about 1750, the year Bach died. Some of the composers are Bach, Telemann, Vivaldi, Handel, and Pachelbel. The term "largo" refers to the tempo. Largos typically range from forty to sixty-five beats per minute.

Use of baroque largos is not arbitrary or a matter of personal taste. Research by Lozanov, the SALT organization, and individual accelerated-learning specialists has verified that this music is the most effective. Sheila Ostrander and Lynn Schroeder, authors of *Superlearning*, also recommend primarily string instruments for the music.

You can put together a music tape by going to a music library, picking out baroque record albums, and using those selections clearly labeled "largo." The only tricky thing is the tempo. Most largos are not exactly sixty beats per minute, so you need to time the music and pick out selections close to this tempo.

If you don't want to record on your own tape, the Learning Power tape available from Powerlearning® Systems has twenty-five minutes of baroque largos performed at exactly sixty beats per minute on side one. The last five minutes of this tape have baroque music that is a little faster. You can rerecord this faster music for a minute or two at the end of your memory tape. This serves as transition from the concert review back into activity.

The concert review requires two tape recorders if you are doing it by yourself. One plays the material you have set up in lexical units. The second plays the baroque largos at sixty beats per minute. You set the two at about the same volume; sit in a nice, comfortable chair; close your eyes; and do the breathing pattern if you have short lexical units, or just relax for extended units. If you have one to two minutes blank at the beginning of your study tape, the music from your second recorder will provide a soothing introduction by itself. The whole process is designed to settle you into a state of restful awareness. When the list ends, shut off the baroque largo tape, and your memory tape will end with a minute or two of the faster baroque music you have recorded.

When people first experience this process, they usually find it easy and relaxing, but the breathing may seem awkward. Be aware that this breathing pattern is unusual and that you should not breathe too deeply while doing it.

Learning the breathing technique recommended here is somewhat like learning to play a new musical instrument, or perhaps learning a new tennis stroke that feels awkward at first and simply requires practice. If you learned to drive with a stick shift, think back to your first time out. Do you remember trying to work the gas pedal here, the clutch over there, and the brake in another place while shifting gears with your hand? It was probably awkward, and you may even have wondered how you could possibly look through the windshield while doing all that. Pretty soon, though, you were driving down the road, working the pedals, shifting the gears, listening to the radio, talking with the friend next to you, watching the highway, and maybe even thinking about something else. The whole process became unconscious. The breathing process is something like that—it's just a matter of practice.

You can do the concert review without doing the breathing pattern; however, it seems to facilitate learning short lexical units. In fact, research suggests that the breathing pattern by itself may improve memory by 78 percent.[6] However, it doesn't seem to help with extended lexical units.

Research[7] at London University using brain-scanning tomography shows clearly that listening to words stimulates more activity in the left side of the brain, where as listening to music stimulates more activity in the right brain. The orchestrated combination in the concert review promotes balanced functioning of the two sides.

When you first experience a concert review, you may notice that the whole process centers on rhythm: You have the material in a rhythm . . . the music supports that rhythm . . . and you may even breathe in rhythm. The continual monotonous rhythm is what lulls you into a relaxed state of restful awareness.

The concert review typically lasts about ten to fifteen minutes. If you figure it out mathematically, in ten minutes you will cover sixty-seven lexical units. That means sixty-seven foreign words or phrases, sixty-seven bones and muscles, sixty-seven technical terms, sixty-seven equations, or sixty-seven of the most difficult-to-remember main points from your review session. That is a lot of material to commit to memory all at once, so I think you can begin to sense the power of this technology.

THE CONCERT REVIEW

- Play the tape with your lexical units, or have a friend read the units aloud.
- Play the baroque largos on a second recorder (your better-quality recorder). Set the two at about the same volume.
- As soon as you start the recorders playing, take your shoes off, put your feet up, and relax in that comfortable chair.
- The two minutes of silence at the start of the memory tape allow for a musical introduction on the other recorder. A friend reading the material should also allow the music to play for two minutes before starting to read.

THE CONCERT REVIEW (continued)

- Close your eyes and listen to the material. For short lexical units you can also incorporate the breathing pattern.
- When the material has finished, shut off the largo tape. If you have ended the material with a minute or two of faster baroque music, this will complete your concert session.

STEP SIX: FEEDBACK

This last step in the cycle is a self-quiz to verify how much of the material you have mastered and that the system really works. You may also discover some material you need to review. As your success grows, this will reinforce the internal suggestion portion of state, the first step. You won't be taking the system on faith because you will have the experience of how effectively it works.

HOW BEST TO USE SUPERMEMORY METHODS

The whole six-step cycle takes one to two hours to complete, depending on how much material you want to absorb at once. Intensive foreign-language courses set up in the Lozanov format are often structured to meet four hours a day. Using these methods, students are able to learn and retain at two to five times the rate of traditional courses.

You might wonder about the best way to use supermemory. I suggest using this technology only for your most difficult *memory* material. If you can simply read through a chapter a few times and have it down, why do all the work of making tapes and doing the six steps? It's not going to save you time.

The whole idea of these methods is to save time and make things easier. If you wanted to learn 150 or 200 German words in one day, you can easily do that using this method. Even with the time it will take you to organize the list, set up your lexical units, record on the tape, and complete the six steps, you can still learn two to five times faster than with any other method of learning.

In my seminars I demonstrate supermemory by having students learn Portuguese vocabulary words at a rate of 80 to 100 words per hour. Afterward, students remember an average of 85 to 90 percent of the words. Sometimes students will come back two or three months after the class and tell me they still remember most of the words.

In the summer of 1975, Ray Benitez-Borden,[8] one of the founders of the SALT Society, conducted several one-year Spanish courses. Each class met four hours a day for ten days—a seven-to-one speedup over traditional techniques and probably the best speedup we've experienced in this country.

Dr. Lin Doherty[9] taught German at the University of Massachusetts for a number of years using Lozanov's Suggestopedia. He taught two years of German in one quarter and had the students put on a dramatic production at the end of the course. That is something a normal language major could not do at the end of four years.

PART FOUR

*L*EARNING

*S*TATES

CHAPTER NINE

POWERREADING

> *Every problem offers a gift.*
> *Am I willing to accept it?*
> —*ANONYMOUS*

Most speed-reading courses don't work. As a typical example, Janet, a physical therapist, knew she should keep up with reading current research in her field, but she felt bogged down with long work hours, and learning business skills to establish her practice. Also, she was not a very good reader. A local speed-reading course promised benefits that looked like they would solve her problems, so she signed up.

For a while some of her reading skills improved, especially reading light fiction. At the conclusion of the course, however, she was disappointed that the course did not live up to the claims. In fact, within a few months her reading skills had slid back to her former level.

It has been estimated that 90 percent of books and courses on reading skills and speed reading—including university courses—make claims that directly contradict the scientific evidence. This chapter is a collection of reading techniques that do work. They also require the least amount of practice to master.

READING PROBLEMS

Many people dislike reading, despite its extreme importance to business, education, and leisure activity. Generally, skilled readers enjoy reading, and poor readers don't. The problem is that most of us were taught enough basic skills to get through school, but few of us learned advanced techniques for speed, comprehension, and recall. Those of us who read slowly and ineffectively are penalized throughout life. We can't keep up with the enormous volume of reading necessary for higher education or staying on top of the latest developments in our field.

EXERCISE 21

Take sixty seconds to list all the things you don't like about reading. Work quickly and list as many as you can think of. When the sixty seconds are over, take another thirty seconds to review the list, make changes, and add new items. *Stop reading* until you have completed this.

Here are what my seminar participants generally dislike about reading; see if any of these things are on your list:

- I read too slowly.
- I am easily distracted.
- My attention wanders.
- I have too much to read and too little time.
- The material is boring!
- I lack comprehension.
- I have trouble concentrating.
- I tend to reread the text too much.

Another problem is illustrated in Figure 9.1. This reader is reading just one word at a time. When she gets to "possible," she thinks,

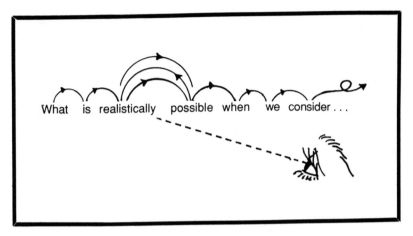

FIGURE 9.1

"Oh, what was that last word?" Her eyes jump back to "realistically." This is called backskipping. Children backskip 25 to 33 percent of the time; adults backskip on 15 percent of the words they read; and even highly efficient readers backskip 5 to 10 percent of the time. This habit, of course, slows reading speed considerably and disrupts the flow of ideas.

One final problem: have you ever noticed that after reading two or three pages, nothing seems to have registered? In northern California we have a technical term for this phenomenon: "spacing out."

When the reader in our illustration gets to "consider," she spaces out. Her eyes move away from the sentence. This may be due to external distractions, boredom, or perhaps contemplating that strawberry short-cake in the refrigerator. Finally, after twenty seconds she remembers, "Oh, I'm supposed to be reading!" But even after those twenty seconds, she back skips to find her place.

EMPOWERING READING STATES

To set up an appropriate state for better reading, you might start with your IR's. Imagine what it would be like if you could significantly improve your reading speed, comprehension, focus, and recall. Also imagine that it would not take a lot of time and energy. How would you *feel* about yourself, and what would you want to read? Can you *picture* yourself being more confident and successful? Would you be *hearing* words encouragement and congratulations? — *SELF-TALK !*

EXERCISE 22

Now take about sixty seconds to list all the benefits you will gain from improved reading. These could tie in with your job, your personal life, or your education. Again, write down all the possible gains as quickly as you can. When the sixty seconds are up, take another thirty seconds to look over the list for additions and refinements. Stop reading until you have completed this.

Here are a few possibilities:

- I could read more in less time.
- I would have more fun reading.
- If reading were easier and more enjoyable, I would learn new things and expand my horizons.
- I would have more knowledge to share with my friends.
- I could finally keep up with the professional reading I'm supposed to do.
- Studying wouldn't take up all of my spare time.
- *QUENCH THIRST FOR KNOWLEDGE*

Reading is power. We acquire most of our knowledge through reading books, magazines, newspapers, reports, and journal articles, as well as an occasional sweet escape to the land of exciting fiction. Improved reading skills is the logical starting point to gain knowledge.

EYE MOVEMENT WHILE READING

Improved reading has a lot to do with how we move our eyes as we read. My seminar participants find it fascinating to observe other readers' eye movements.

EXERCISE 23

Closely watch a friend's eyes while he or she is reading. You will observe a fine jerky motion as the friend stops on each word momentarily and then jerks to the next. In fact, if you watch carefully, you may observe occasional backskipping.

The time we spend stopping on each word is called a *fixation*. For most of us, fixations last one-quarter to one-half second. The quick jerks from one fixation point to the next are called *sacades*.

We can scientifically study patterns of eye movement by taking a narrow beam of light and bouncing it from the eye of a reader onto a piece of photographic film. As the reader's eye moves across the line of print, the light reflected from his or her eye moves across the film. If the film is also moving during the process, we can record the pattern of fixations and sacades. *Eye movement photography* research has been done for the past sixty years, and much of our present scientific understanding of reading skills is based on this research.

Figure 9.2 shows a reader who, at this moment, is fixating on the letter "l."

Only two or three letters to either side of this fixation point are entirely in focus. This is the shaded region—the area of 100 percent visual acuity. At one-half inch to either side of the fixation point, clarity is reduced to 30 percent. Beyond that the letters are out of focus and thus indecipherable.

Most people are surprised at how narrow our region of sharp vision really is. Because of this, we cannot take in an entire line of print at once. We gradually move across it, momentarily putting each part within our narrow field of sharp vision.

Another fact we have learned from eye movement photography is that the typical reader takes in an average of only 1.1 words with each stop or fixation. The best readers take in 2.5 words with each stop. Beyond 2.5 words, the print appears too distorted to recognize.

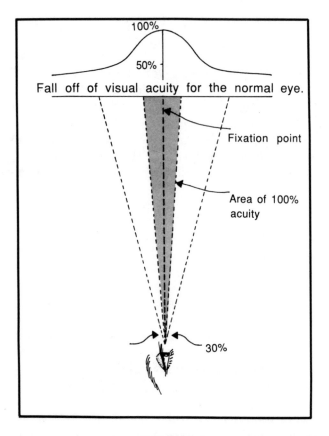

FIGURE 9.2

SPEED-READING FACT AND FICTION

How much can you improve your reading skills if you practice the exercises presented later in this chapter? What speeds are possible? What claims are realistic? Here are the most common misconceptions:

1. *Possible reading speeds.* Many of the commercial speed-reading courses claim possible reading speeds from 1,000 to 80,000 words per minute. However, if you figure it out mathemati-

cally, the best reader spends about 0.25 second with each fixation and takes in about 2.5 words. That sets a practical speed limit of 800 to 900 words per minute if you are going to see each word. And you do have to see each word to understand everything except light fiction.

No doubt there are exceptions. John F. Kennedy reportedly could read a newspaper at 2,000 words per minute. Once in a while you hear of people with photographic memories who look at a page once and have it down. However, for the average person, 800 to 900 words per minute seems to be the practical limit. On the other hand, if you can reach even 500 words per minute, that's still better than the vast majority of readers. As you will discover, these levels are not difficult to reach. Exercises in Appendix Two, "Your Sixty-Day Reading Program," will provide you with the vehicle to increase your reading speed.

2. *Phrase reading.* Almost every book on speed reading and every course on the subject will tell you not to read one word at a time. With each stop or fixation, you are advised to take in a whole phrase. This is inconsistent with eye movement photography that shows the very best readers take in no more than 2.5 words with each stop or fixation.

Commercial and university courses train students to expand their side or *peripheral* vision with a device called a *phrase flashing machine.* The student stares straight ahead at a screen, and the machine flashes a phrase or a short sentence in a short fraction of a second. With a little practice, most people can take in the whole line that quickly. The line is in fact considerably longer than 2.5 words.

The catch, however, is this: When you read, your eyes are moving and not just staring straight ahead. Once your eyes move, you have a much narrower field of visual acuity.

There are some "phrase flashing" exercises in Appendix Two. They are useful for expanding your peripheral vision. Using these exercises can enhance your skills from the usual 1.1 words per fixation to the peak performance level of 2.5 words with each stop. It is very unlikely, however, that you will take in an entire phrase at a time while reading.

3. *Eliminate backskipping.* Almost all speed-reading books and courses will tell you to *eliminate* backskipping. Generally, this is

not possible. While reading, the eyes start and stop so fast (four times per second) that it is almost involuntary where they finally stop. Periodically they will go back, whether you want them to or not. However, you can minimize backskipping simply by increasing your reading speed. The faster your speed (up to a reasonably quick pace), the less tendency there will be to backskip. The *visual aid* technique described later also helps to reduce backskipping.

4. *Speed and appreciation.* The idea here is that "those fast readers don't appreciate the material as much as we slow readers do." I think the slow readers started that rumor. It's just not true. If you're a fast reader, you have more choices. You can slow down and savor something you enjoy. You have time to reread material if you desire. And just knowing that a reading assignment will not take up your whole evening could add appreciation to the process. It's much more enjoyable to have the ability and choice to read faster.

5. *"It's more work to read fast."* This isn't so. Research has shown that faster readers, on average, backskip only about half as much as slow readers. In addition, faster readers do only half as many fixations per line.[1] Now, just think: Your eyes are starting, stopping, moving back, and jumping around four times per second. This is what wears you out as you read. This is also what causes the fatigue, the boredom, and a lack of concentration. If you are a fast reader and your eyes jump around only half as much, you are doing less work yet getting more done.

6. *"The faster the speed, the lower the concentration."* Again, this is not true. A big problem in reading is that our mind works so much faster than the rate at which we are reading. That's why some people get bored with it. It would be like listening to someone speak . . . one . . . word . . . at . . . a . . . time. When we take in information faster, it is easier to concentrate because our reading speed matches the natural rhythm of our mind. A simple analogy would be driving down a residential street at twenty-five miles per hour with your attention wandering, as opposed to driving on a German *Autobahn* at ninety miles per hour with total concentration.

MODELING EXCELLENT READERS

Just now as you are reading notice . . . is this book flat on the table
or on your lap like this,

FIGURE 9.3

or are you holding it upright like this?

FIGURE 9.4

EXERCISE 24: READING PRETEST

Before learning specific techniques of how to improve your reading skills, it is useful to know what your starting level is. To do this you will read an article in Appendix One, time your reading speed, and answer some questions to test your comprehension. Turn to Appendix One and complete this pretest *now* before continuing to the next section.

When people read at my seminars, 90 percent of them have their book flat on their desk or on their lap, as in Figure 9.3. Only 10 percent hold the book upright, as in Figure 9.4. Notice what holding the reading material does for your posture: It's more upright. This is a *visual* posture that promotes alertness. By laying the reading material flat on your table or on your lap, notice what happens: Your posture is slouched . . . a kinesthetic pose—a good way to go to sleep.

EXERCISE 25

Now try this for yourself. Go back a page or two and read for a few seconds with the book flat on your lap, desk, or table. Next, hold the book up, place it a comfortable distance from your eyes, and continue reading. See what differences you feel between the two postures.

What happened when you did this exercise? My seminar participants report that after using the more upright position:

- I feel more alert.
- It's easier to breathe.
- I can read faster.

• I feel more connected with what I'm reading.
• The print is easier to see.

Think about this last statement. It's got to be easier to see! If the book is flat, look at your viewing angle to the print.

FIGURE 9.5

When you're holding a book this way, look what happens: The angle, perpendicular to the page, makes the print clearly more visible.

When we model the very best readers, we imitate their physiologies, IR's, and the unconscious keys they use. They generally do two things with their physiologies (K^e);[2] They:

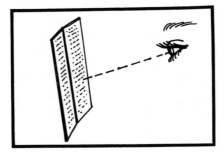

FIGURE 9.6

• hold the material with a visual posture
• use a visual aid

Of course, holding the material can be difficult with some textbooks that feel like they weigh ninety pounds. But with a heavy book, you can get a book holder to place on your table or desk. This will give you the proper viewing angle. You can still hold on to the material for that sense of connection.

A visual aid could be your finger, a pen, or better, a pencil. Move the pencil underneath the line you are reading. Don't underline, just move the pencil. If you are not using a visual aid as you read this book, try using one right *now*.

FIGURE 9.7

Do you notice any difference?

Some of the most highly skilled readers always have a pencil in their hand as they read. Watch a proofreader. But you may be thinking, "Isn't that what I used to do in elementary school, and the teacher told me not to do it?" That's true. Small children are discouraged from pointing to words as they read. What the teacher ought to do is have them move their fingers faster.

A visual aid provides a point of focus, and we are instinctively drawn to motion. Research done on the simple technique of moving a pencil under the line of print shows that within the first few hours, most people experience a 40 percent reduction in the number of stops per line. Backskipping is reduced by 50 percent, and reading speed jumps 40 to 50 percent. The reduction in backskipping is easy enough to understand. With a pencil moving forward, it is less likely that the eyes will fall back.

YOUR KEY FOR READING EXCELLENCE

One thing I learned quickly when I first started presenting Powerlearning® seminars is that most participants want to improve their reading skills, but very few have the patience or time to do extended training to get results. My motivation then was to provide this key as a collection of simple, practical techniques that require no practice and give immediate improvements. What follows is the result of my research and the experiences of my seminar participants.

1. K^e—*physiology.* This, as we discussed in the previous section, is modeling the way excellent readers hold the material (or use a book holder) for a visual posture and use a visual aid.

2. *Right brain.* Involve the right brain more through *prereading.* Many of the steps in the key will promote higher speed when you read. Equally important, however, is the ability to *focus* and *comprehend.* Prereading is an important tool toward that end.

Prereading can take a number of different forms. One simple approach is to read the first sentence of each paragraph of a book chapter the first time through. If it's a long paragraph, reading the first two sentences might be better. Exceptions would be the introduction, summaries, and conclusions. Read these thoroughly.

Within five or ten minutes you'll be all the way through the chapter and have a pretty good idea what it's about—without reading very many words. This allows you to begin *seeing the whole picture* of the material, a right-brain approach. Now when you go back and speed-read (a more left-brain activity), you'll have a mental skeleton to put things together. This makes it easier to focus and concentrate.

One exception to this prereading approach occurs when you are reading difficult or technical material. In this case, read everything the first time through. See each word, each equation, each chart or graph without being concerned about whether you understand it. That is very difficult for many of us. We refuse to move to page 2 unless we have completely understood page 1. You need to trust that you are working on it unconsciously. The material gradually makes more sense on the second or third reading.

3. V^e—*optimize the quality of visual input.* As we discussed, holding the material improves the viewing angle, and the visual aid provides a moving point of focus. Of course, proper lighting is important here. Beyond this, four strategies provide optimal visual input:

- *Use high-speed practice.* Suppose you were riding in a high-speed train at ninety miles per hour. You travel at this speed for half an hour, so you get used to it. Then the train begins slowing down for the station up ahead, and the passenger next to you estimates that you are now traveling at thirty-five miles per hour. The average person would probably estimate thirty-five miles per hour when the train is actually moving at forty-five to fifty-five miles per hour. This is because they've acclimated to the moving rate of ninety miles per hour as opposed to a highway speed of fifty-five to sixty-five miles per hour.

Reading at high speeds is a similar phenomenon. One of the exercises in Appendix Two for improving your reading speed is to spend ten to fifteen minutes a day reading considerably faster than your normal speed. Don't worry about seeing all the words or having total comprehension; just get used to reading faster. Afterward, return to your normal reading speed and watch what happens: Your speed will spontaneously begin to increase.

• *Shorten the lines by one-half inch on each side.* Take your visual aid (pencil) and put a vertical line on each side of the page about one-half inch from the margin.

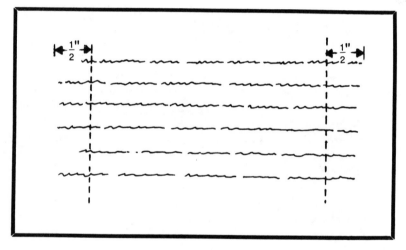

FIGURE 9.8

Draw the lines very lightly so you can erase them easily later without damaging the book. Now move under the line of print with your pencil, but stay between the two vertical lines. You won't miss the outside words; you'll pick them up with your peripheral vision.

It's much easier to read across short lines with a smooth, consistent rhythm than longer lines. Perhaps this is why newspaper lines are so short. With practice you won't have to draw in your vertical lines. You'll know to start one-half inch from one margin and end one-half inch before the next.

• *Expand fixation size.* Work to develop your peripheral side vision. Here is a way to demonstrate the quality of your peripheral vision:

Put your arm out straight in front of you. While looking

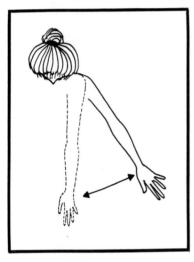

straight ahead, rotate your arm by about forty-five degrees, back toward your side. Now, at a forty-five-degree angle, raise one finger, then two, then three, etc. You will probably see the movement, but I doubt that you can count the number of fingers going up. Our peripheral vision is very poorly developed, except for movement.

With proper training, though, you can significantly improve your peripheral vision. It will never be as clear as your central vision because of the structure of the retina.

FIGURE 9.9

Your peripheral vision can, however, certainly be improved and expanded. A good step in this direction is the "phrase flashing exercises" described in Appendix Two. With practice you can expand your potential from the usual 1.1 words per fixation to the best: 2.5 words per stop.

• *Learn to vary your reading speed.* You might experience that when you read for pleasure, you go considerably faster than for technical reading. It's likely that you do vary your speed somewhat, but probably not as much as you think. The average person varies his or her reading speed by only 10 percent and should have a much larger range that that. You should be able to vary from 100 or 150 words per minute for difficult reading, up to 800 to 900 words per minute for lighter fiction.

Just be aware that your speed should naturally vary from subject to subject. Using techniques in this key, you can speed up any type of reading, but you will never read *Calculus IV* at the same rate as *Reader's Digest*.

4. A[i]—*eliminate subvocalizing.* Do this for nontechnical or lighter reading. Subvocalizing is that little voice inside your head that allows you to hear the words as you see them. Some people even move their lips or whisper the words as they read.

Where did that voice come from? It probably started in your first grade of elementary school. Most of us were taught to read aloud. Then we learned to read to ourselves. Then the teacher hoped that little voice would go away. Guess what? After all these years, it's probably still there.

We usually assume we need to hear the material to understand and remember it. When people take speed-reading courses and read the words without hearing them, they initially feel they don't remember what they read. When they are tested on the material, however, it is there.

As we have discussed, visual memory is more reliable than auditory memory for most people. Recall without subvocalizing is through a visual link instead of the more familiar auditory loop. Subvocalization keeps our reading speed under about three hundred words per minute. The fact that the little voice can't talk any faster than three hundred words per minute creates a barrier to reaching higher speeds.

There are several ways to get rid of that little voice.

- One way many people find helpful is *knuckle-biting.* As you read, bite down lightly on a knuckle of the hand you do not write with—you may be moving your visual aid with the writing hand. The idea of biting down on something is to throw the muscles associated with speech off balance. This makes it easier to remind yourself to let go of the voice.

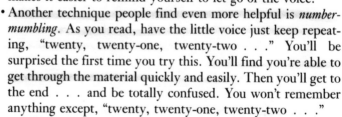

- Another technique people find even more helpful is *number-mumbling.* As you read, have the little voice just keep repeating, "twenty, twenty-one, twenty-two . . ." You'll be surprised the first time you try this. You'll find you're able to get through the material quickly and easily. Then you'll get to the end . . . and be totally confused. You won't remember anything except, "twenty, twenty-one, twenty-two . . ."

With a little practice, though, you will begin absorbing the material without hearing it. All you are hearing is the numbers. Finally the voice gets bored with the numbers and it stops. At this point your reading speed may jump ahead quickly. When you get beyond three hundred words per minute, the voice can't keep up, so you won't have a subvocalizing problem. However, keep in mind that hearing the numbers is just a temporary method to help you reach higher speeds.

- The third technique is *reading at higher speeds*. Test your reading speed. If you read under three hundred words per minute, subvocalization may be holding you back. If you read beyond three hundred words per minute, you don't have a subvocalization problem, so don't worry about it.

5. A^i—*use subvocalizing*. Do this for difficult or technical reading. At this point it is good to make a distinction between reading and study. When trying to understand and remember difficult material, it's useful to see it, hear it, write it, and cover all the senses. When we discuss reading, however, we've been talking about that first exposure, where you simply need to see the words and take them in. — *PreRead Practice*

We also distinguish between light reading and difficult or technical material. If the material is especially difficult or technical, we can't go faster than three hundred words per minute, so don't worry about subvocalizing. In fact, there is a school of thought that believes that during difficult reading it is better to have the little voice carrying on an internal dialogue—questioning, anticipating, and massaging the material. It is primarily for lighter reading, where there are many pages or chapters to cover, that it's not necessary to hear the words.

6. K^i—*learn to derive more pleasure from reading*. You, too, will gain confidence and pleasure with reading as you incorporate this key. If you don't feel initially motivated to read, imagine what it would be like if you were. How would you be sitting? How would your body feel? How would things look? Even if you initially just pretend you are motivated, this is often enough to get you started and make the process more pleasurable.

In summary, your reading key is shown in Figure 9.10

The simple techniques and modeling in this key increased my reading speed to five hundred words per minute. This is

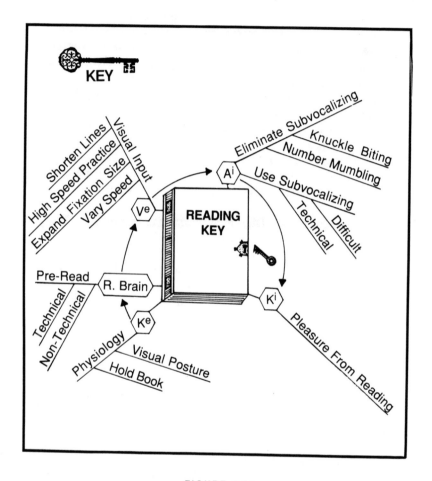

FIGURE 9.10

still better than the vast majority of our population. But if you really want to go for it—that is, if you want to reach the practical reading speed limit of eight hundred to nine hundred words per minute—use the collection of exercises in "Your Sixty-Day Reading Program" in Appendix Two.

EXERCISE 26: AFTERTEST

Once you have been using the techniques from the key for a week or two, you may want to check your progress against your previous pretest. As before, you will read an article, time your reading speed, and answer some questions to check your comprehension. Turn to Appendix Three for the aftertest.

CHAPTER TEN

POWERSTUDY

> When I works, I works hard;
> When I sits, I sits loose;
> When I thinks, I falls asleep.
> —ANONYMOUS

The average university student is expected to spend about two thousand hours in class and another four thousand hours studying. That is equivalent to about forty hours per week of solid study for two years. Furthermore, high schools and universities assume that good study skills come naturally for students and make little attempt to teach students how to study and learn more effectively. As students we do the best we can and hope our strategies will work. Unfortunately, it's often not enough.

In this chapter we will examine strategies to overcome barriers to effective study and learning. These include getting started, remembering what we have read and studied, getting the most from study time, and improving understanding.

REMEMBERING WHAT YOU'VE READ AND STUDIED

Diane enjoyed showing off her custom home—a benefit of her years of study to become a successful lawyer. She especially enjoyed showing off her study with its impressive library of books, texts, and references. One evening after her friends had left, she wandered back into the library and had a strange thought: "I wonder what's in all the books I've read throughout my life." Of course, she knew generally what was there, but she wondered if she still remembered one tenth or even one hundredth of everything she had studied. I wonder if you have ever had a similar feeling.

An important part of reading and study is remembering it. This falls into two categories: remembering material from each part of a class or study session, and remembering material altogether after the class or study session is over. Memory from each part of a class or study session follows the Ebbinghaus curve we discussed in Chapter Six.

The shape of the curve in Figure 10.1 shows two peak memory times. The primacy effect shows best recall from the beginning of a study session, and the recency effect shows additional high recall at the end. This particular student remembered about 70 percent from the beginning of his study session. After three hours of solid study, however, his recall was down to only about 30 percent.

If he had taken a break after two hours, the recency effect could have increased the recall as shown in Figure 10.2.

Even so, he can still recall only about 40 percent of what he is studying by the end of two hours. Both these curves show unfortunate results, because they show that we study best at the beginning, when we are freshest. Isn't there some way to keep recall at the high level we start with?

REMEMBER TO BREAK! VERY IMPORTANT

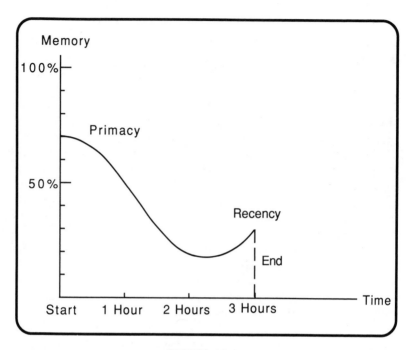

FIGURE 10.1

MODULAR STUDY

The trick to maximizing recall from a class or study session without having to employ the memory techniques from Chapters Six through Eight is to downchunk the material into modules: *modular study*. The German researcher B. Zeigarnik[1] surmised that the shorter the study session or class, the less the drop in memory, and the more relative benefit from the reminiscent effect. However, if the session is too short, downchunking inhibits seeing the broader whole picture, and the unit lacks sufficient meaning. If it is too long, recall and efficiency drop off. Many researchers[2] have observed that interrupting an extended learning session with a break at just the right time enhances memory and effectiveness.

Ideally, then, you should take a break every thirty to forty minutes. I did not say take a thirty- or forty-minute break; five to ten minutes is

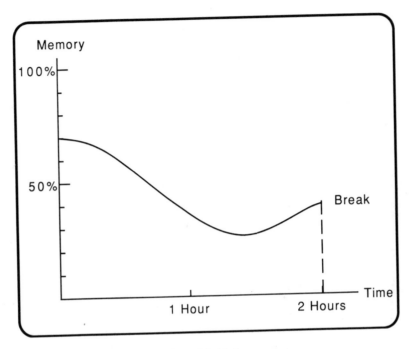

FIGURE 10.2

enough. That's enough time to stand up and stretch, splash some water on your face, or get a snack or some fresh air. The break should be relaxing and totally different from your session activity. (See the "Break Time Activities" box.) If the student in Figures 10.1 and 10.2 used this modular study with breaks, the memory curve would probably look more like that shown in Figure 10.3.

You can use this routine for hours because it helps maintain a high level of recall, and it also keeps your energy at a high level. The same is true on your job. A change of pace every thirty to forty minutes enhances efficiency.

On the other hand, suppose you are studying something especially difficult, such as advanced calculus. Perhaps you have been studying for two hours and it just isn't making any sense, when suddenly it starts falling into place. At this point, should you take a break, or keep going with your momentum? Many people guess that you should keep going a while longer to get into the flow. That's not the right answer. It would be better to take a break.

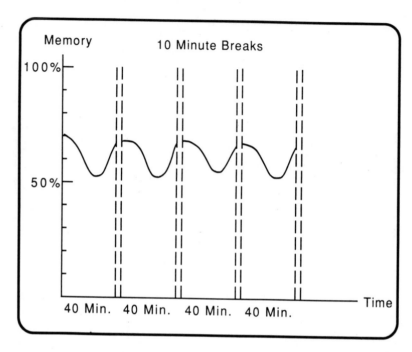

FIGURE 10.3

If you keep going, you may understand the material, but it's less likely that you will remember it. Haven't you had situations where you understood something, but on the test you couldn't remember it? Ideally, you want to have both understanding and memory. If you take a break, you'll look forward to coming back because you were starting to get the material, and now it is more likely you will remember it.

BREAK-TIME ACTIVITIES

During my five- to ten-minute breaks every thirty to forty minutes, I usually do several of the following:

• splash a little cold water on my face
• do a few minutes of stretching exercises
• get something to drink or a piece of fruit
• lie with my eyes closed for a few minutes
• step outside for some fresh air and sunshine
• juggle
• dance

Juggling is excellent during a break because it promotes mind-body coordination, promotes left-brain/right-brain balance, and provides a good metaphor for all we have to do in life. I teach juggling in my two-day seminars. Also, most novelty shops carry a kit called "Juggling for the Complete Klutz"—an easy way to start.

LONG-TERM MEMORY

Taking a break every thirty to forty minutes will help maximize recall from each part of a class or study session, but what about holding on to the recall long after the class or study session is over? Without reenforcement, recall might fall off along the general shape of an Ebbinghaus curve as shown in Figure 10.4.

For this particular student, recall increases slightly for about ten minutes after the study session—again illustrating the reminiscent effect. Then it falls off. After twenty-four hours, recall is about 70 percent gone, and from there it gradually disappears. However, there are two ways to keep the recall at the high level it was at the end of your study session: a series of four to five reviews, or a supermemory concert review.

Ten minutes after your class or study session and just after your

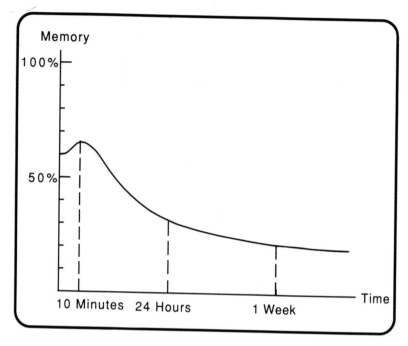

FIGURE 10.4

break, take your first review. This consists of rereading and revising your notes. For an hour's worth of class or study time, you might take five to ten minutes to reread and revise your notes. This ten-minute period is crucial in transferring information from short-term to long-term memory. Revising your notes might also take the form of organizing the information into a pattern discovery map. This technique always helps you to pull the information together to see the whole picture (V^i and right brain). Writing out the pattern discovery map also promotes kinesthetic involvement (K^e).

Take your second review one day later—after you have had a chance to process the material with a night's sleep. This time list the main points you learned twenty-four hours ago from memory—not all the detail, just the main headings or main points. Compare these with your original notes to see if you left anything out. Then add any missing main points. This second review might take another four to five minutes and should be sufficient to bring back the rest of the detail of what you learned.

Take your third review one week after the class or study session.

Follow the same procedure as your second review: Recall from memory the main points or headings you learned one week ago, and compare with your notes. This will take another five minutes or so.

The fourth and possibly last review occurs one month after the initial session and is just like the second and third reviews. It will take only four to five minutes. As an option, you can review the information again in six months; you'll probably find it is still there.

At this point you have invested a total review time of twenty to thirty minutes, which is very efficient to learn and retain an hour's worth of study material. Of course, you may be thinking that if you are taking four or five classes and try to schedule four or five reviews for each class, you could get into some serious bookkeeping problems. In this case I suggest leaving space between your classes if at all possible. In this way you can do the first review 10 minutes after each class.

For your second review, you might want to lump all of today's classes together and review them tomorrow in one sitting. Again, a week from today schedule a third review for all of today's classes. You can schedule the one-month review and the six-month review in the same way.

The forgetting curve without the reviews is now modified to look as shown in Figure 10.5.

For this student, the reviews added 30 to 40 percent to the study time but improved recall by 500 percent! This is a typical result and definitely not a bad investment of time. It would be like investing thirty-five hundred dollars to get back fifty thousand dollars!

If the material is particularly difficult to remember or if you are in a hurry to commit it to long-term memory, there is an alternative method to the reviews. Make a tape of the material in lexical units and do the six-step supermemory process outlined in Chapter Eight. In this way you don't have to extend your reviews over a longer time. If the material is not so difficult to remember, but perhaps you have a large volume of it, the four reviews would probably be easier. In that way you don't have to make a tape.

STUDY: YOUR KEY TO GETTING STARTED

The two biggest complaints I hear about study are (1) procrastination and (2) having enough time to study once you finally stop procrasti-

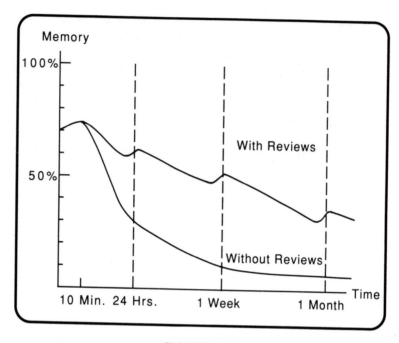

FIGURE 10.5

nating. Many of us have elaborate rituals to get started—a cup of coffee, spring-cleaning the room we'll be studying in, a walk to the store for a snack, or a nap. Of course, these provide ways to keep busy without getting anything done.

EXERCISE 27

Take a minute or two to list the things you don't like or perhaps find difficult about study. Go for quantity. Once you have the list, pick the three or four items that are most difficult for you. Stop reading until you have completed this.

My seminar participants frequently report the following. Are any of these on your list?

EXERCISE 27 (continued)

- I don't feel motivated to study.
- It's too much work.
- Study is boring.
- I have too many other things I'd rather be doing.
- It's a sure way to fall asleep.

The best way to ensure the success of a study session is to set up a brief study preparation phase. If you are having a hard time getting started, you might start with supermemory step 1—*State*. A few stretching exercises, physical relaxation, and internal suggestions can ease you into a more empowering state within about five minutes. On the other hand, if you're all fired up and can hardly wait to study, skip this step.

EXERCISE 28

Think back to a time when you were totally motivated to study and you were focused on and effective with that study. Think of a *specific* time and be back in that situation. Notice as much visual, auditory, and kinesthetic detail as you can. If you can't remember a specific time, just imagine what it would be like if you did have that focus and motivation.

Now take a few minutes to list personal benefits you would derive from being able to study this effectively. What changes would you be able to make in your life? How would you feel about yourself? How would you feel about new learning?

VISUALIZE AND MAKE BELIEVE IF NO MEMORIES COME TO MIND.

Many people have a hard time getting motivated to study because they hear a stern voice inside (A^i) telling them they *should* be studying now, or they *have to* start working on the assignment right away. They picture (V^i) what will happen if they don't do it. Their resulting state is a rebellion against that stern voice and feeling paralyzed by seeing the prospect of failure. A more useful approach is to use your motivation key from Chapter Two.

Once you have established an empowering state, the magic key shown in Figure 10.6 will help prepare you to get the most from your study time.

Let's go through this step by step:

1. K^e—*physiology*. A first consideration in preparing yourself to study is to make sure your environment will support focus and effective learning. The best temperature for study is cool enough to avoid drowsiness. A back support for the lower back promotes an alert visual posture and eases tension.

2. V^e—*optimize visual input*. Do this as you do with reading. The most ideal lighting is indirect solar light, coming from a window, outdoor shade, or a frosted skylight. At night, incandescent light is okay. Fluorescent is the worst form of lighting for this purpose.[5] Its spectrum is so distorted from natural sunlight that it promotes fatigue and makes it hard to concentrate. Studies show that fluorescent light even promotes hyperactivity in young children.

3. A^e—*minimize noise and distractions*. Setting up an environment free from distractions and interruptions improves focus and concentration. Agreement with roommates or family about quiet times for study is helpful.

4. Left brain—*decide the time and scope of material to cover*. Perhaps it's now 7:00 P.M., so you decide to study until 7:40 P.M. (Remember that thirty to forty minutes is the ideal length for a class or study session.) You might decide that one chapter in a text is a reasonable amount of material for your study session. You can even put a marker at the beginning and the end of the chapter. When you are that clear with your goals, the mind has a strong tendency to complete them.

5. A^i—*internal dialogue*. Take a minute or two to ask yourself what you already know about the material and what you would like to know when you are done. Maybe you'd like to know the

ANY LONGER TAKE A BREAK

→ *DECIDE AND FORM INTENT!*

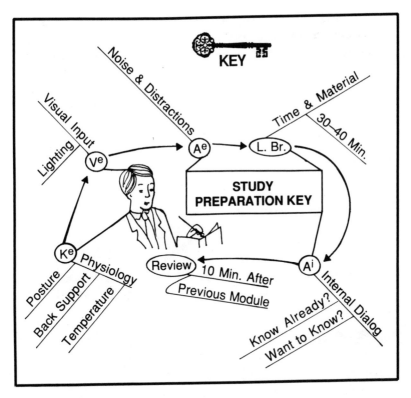

FIGURE 10.6

answers to the questions at the end of your chapter. Read the questions first. Even though they make no sense now, as you read through the chapter, the important points will jump out at you.

Another way to accomplish this is to glance through the chapter, take each section heading, and turn it into a question. As an example, if you are reading through an introductory chapter on physics and the first section is "Momentum," your question might be, "What is momentum, and what does it mean physically?" Maybe the next section is "Kinetic Energy." Your question might be, "What is kinetic energy, and does it relate to momentum?" This process actively involves you in the study.

6. Review. The last step is to *review* what you were doing just before the last break. Remember the ten-minute review from the previous section? It's a great idea to employ your super-

memory techniques from time to time during your study session. Then, tomorrow, twenty-four hours after your review, you'll have your study material in your long-term memory.

Beyond this key, having a routine time and place for study is freeing because you don't have to decide when and where to study. Of course, all of this is common sense, and I find that better students tend to incorporate some of these ideas instinctively. It is likely that if you follow these steps you will be more focused and effective and require less study time.

GETTING THE MOST FROM YOUR STUDY TIME

After the preparation, I recommend a four-step process for study. The technique is to go through the material four times, but reread only a fraction of the words[6].

1. *Visual preview.* If you need to study a book, glance through the whole book very quickly—the back cover, contents, preface, and introduction. Quickly thumb through the book to pick up pictures, a few headings, and to get a general idea of what it looks like—as though you were browsing in a bookstore. For a chapter or article, glance through the headings, the subheadings, illustrations, graphs, charts, and footnotes—not to understand them but just to see what they look like.

2. *Reading preview.* For an article or a chapter, go all the way through, reading the first one or two sentences of each paragraph. Along with this, read the introductions, summaries, and conclusions thoroughly. In Chapter Nine, this is what we call prereading. If you have not already done so, read the questions at the end of your chapter and turn section titles into questions. For technical information or difficult reading, read everything without trying to understand it the first time through.

   For a whole book, preread and read the first chapter. Then preread any internal chapter that seems to be a summary or transition, then read it thoroughly. Finally, preread and read the last chapter thoroughly.

3. *Study view.* Now go back and read the rest of the words with a deeper level of understanding. Skip or skim sections that seem unimportant. When you come to important sections, mark them with your visual aid (a soft pencil) as shown in Figure 10.7.

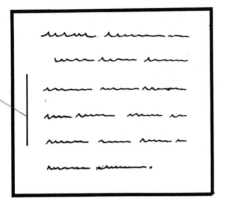

FIGURE 10.7

For sections that are confusing or difficult, mark them as shown in Figure 10.8

Do not underline or highlight the material—that is much too slow. For difficult or confusing material, don't stop or get bogged down. What is confusing on page 3 may be better explained on page 5. It would be a waste of time to get slowed down just now, but note for later reference the fact that it was confusing.

FIGURE 10.8

4. *Afterview and note-taking.* Go back only to those sections you marked as important or confusing, and now start taking notes. Many people take notes the first time through, without knowing what's important or not important. They usually take notes on everything. If you wait until later, you will see the important points and the confusing points. You will also have more of a vision of the whole. At this point you can likely reduce your volume of notes by 60 to 70 percent. Also, if you want to, set up your notes in pattern discovery map formats.

To secure what you have studied in long-term memory, follow the guidelines earlier in this chapter. Review your material ten minutes later, twenty-four hours later, a week later, a month later, and perhaps six months later. If something is particularly difficult to remember, use memory strategies from Chapters Six and Seven, or record a tape in lexical units and do a concert review of the material.

It is good to begin your study time with the most difficult or boring material—what you least want to do. You might also alternate contrasting subjects to maintain variety and interest.

If you have used elaborate rituals such as a cup of coffee, listening to music, or a walk to get yourself started, save these for break-time rewards, or rewards for when you have completed your study. It is also important to avoid marathon study sessions. These drain your energy, anchor stress and panic with learning, and aren't particularly effective.

REWARD LIST FOR STUDY

Here are some activities you might reward yourself with at various stages of achievement in your studies:

- running or jogging
- drawing
- listening to music
- taking time for your favorite sport
- going to a movie
- writing letters
- acting in a play
- buying new clothes
- meditating
- gardening
- playing with pets
- reading for pleasure
- playing with your kids
- doing yoga exercises
- shopping
- playing a musical instrument
- going to the beach
- taking time to do something you've always wanted to do but never had the time

LEARNING TIPS TO IMPROVE UNDERSTANDING

The methods we've discussed to this point promote good use of your time, ease in getting started with your study, effective reading skills, mental clarity, focus, and ease in remembering what you've read and studied. All this should produce a learning state more conducive to understanding what you've studied. In addition, we can incorporate a few more techniques from NLP to help you understand the more difficult material.

When we model successful students, we find they approach their course work aggressively. They get to know their instructors; they take advantage of office hours and discussion time to clarify their understanding; and they actively participate in class instead of being a passive sponge.

You will usually be most successful understanding difficult material if your initial exposure is in your primary modality—visual, auditory, or kinesthetic. Many instructors rely primarily on auditory presentations, with perhaps a little visual reinforcement. If you are finding the presentation difficult to follow, ask for clarification in your primary modality:

- *Visual:* "Can you help me *visualize* that idea?" or "I can't quite *picture* what you're saying."
- *Auditory:* "That *sounds* confusing to me. It would help to *hear* it in a different way."
- *Kinesthetic:* "Could you make that more *concrete*, so I can get a better *feel* for it (or get more of a *handle* on it)?

Then practice the material on your own, or in a small study group if you can. Be sure to incorporate your primary modality: picturing the ideas (V^i), explaining the concepts to others (A^e), or writing out the principles (K^e).

One final suggestion: Be careful where you sit in the class.[7] If the class favors the right side of your brain, sit on the right side of the class. Examples of right-brain subjects include art; music appreciation; and any class promoting vivid imagery, such as literature or occasionally psychology. Sitting on the right promotes right-brain functioning.

If the class favors the left side of the brain—math, hard science,

English grammar, etc.—sit on the left side. This promotes left-brain functioning. If you want more balance, you might sit in the middle. Students instinctively prefer one side or the other in various classes. If you ask them why, they respond, "I don't know. I just like to sit here," or "I like to sit there." When you see where better students are, you will find a correlation between the side of the room and the type of class. If you aren't sure whether the subject favors one side of the brain more than the other, find out where the better students are sitting. You may want to join them. If it's a crowded class, don't tell everybody what you are doing.

The keys we have gathered for motivation, memory, reading, and study are the most powerful known. Our next step is to unlock barriers to personal power.

PART FIVE

STATES

FOR

PERSONAL

POWER

CHAPTER ELEVEN

*T*HE COLOR OF TIME

> *Today is the tomorrow*
> *you didn't plan for yesterday.*
> —*ANONYMOUS*

In *Powerlearning*® we have focused on developing thinking, memory, and learning skills with the philosophy that achieving the goals, dreams, and states we desire will involve learning. To the extent that we learn more effectively, we gain personal power—the ability to paint our desired destiny on the fabric of life.

We all have three primary colors with which to work: (1) time, (2) living life intelligently, and (3) living life with passion. These are the subjects of our concluding chapters.

INFORMATION OVERLOAD

Beyond air pollution, water pollution, and toxic wastes in our natural environment, most of us are now confronted with a new toxin that discolors our time: *information overload*, often in the form of "paper pollution." When I use the term *information overload*, I wonder if that rings a bell with you. Do you sometimes experience too much to do, not enough time to do it, and a feeling of being overwhelmed?

Below is an artist's conception of information overload. I wonder if you sometimes have days when you feel like the person in the middle of this next picture.

FIGURE 11.1

I'm sure we've all had days like this. From my research I am convinced that the three things that most discolor our available time are lack of knowledge on:

- how to custom-tailor our use of time
- how to manage power flow
- how to reduce or eliminate fatigue

Let's begin with time.

YOUR DIRECTION IN TIME

Time management is the art of making the most of the time we have. This can be crucial for those of us working in more than one job, taking classes, and maintaining family and friends while trying to maintain a balance of recreation and play, keeping up a household, and keeping up with rest and exercise. Life may seem like juggling with too many pieces falling on the floor.

The first step toward effective yet artful use of your time is to know clearly your direction through time. Following are some exercises I first encountered in Alan Laikin's pioneering work *How to Get Control of the Time in Your Life*. If you haven't done exercises like these in the past two or three months, it is very useful to do them *now*.

EXERCISE 29

Take a blank sheet of paper and spend not more than two minutes to list the things you would like to accomplish during the rest of your life. Write as fast as you can, and go for quantity. Be sure to include all of the playful, as well as practical, and even outrageous possibilities, like skydiving or that African safari— whatever you have ever dreamed of doing, even if it didn't seem practical or sensible. Do not spend more than two minutes making the list. Check your clock or watch and start *now*.

Once you have finished, take one more minute to go back over the list for additions or modifications.

EXERCISE 30

Take a second blank sheet of paper and for not more than two minutes list all you would like to do in the next five years. Some of these may be the same as items on your first list, some may be different. Again, go for quantity and avoid censoring the possibilities. When you are ready, *start*.

When the two minutes are up, take one more minute to go back over the list to make additions or changes.

EXERCISE 31

Take a third blank sheet of paper and spend another two minutes on the following. Suppose you knew you would be dead in six months. All of the funeral arrangements and legal matters have been taken care of, and money is not an obstacle. What would you do during these last six months? Again, go for quantity.

Again, once you have completed, spend one more minute to go back over the list to check for possible additions or corrections.

EXERCISE 32

Take one minute each to go back over your three lists in Exercises 29, 30, and 31 and pick the five items from each you would most like to do—the ones that are most dear to you. Start with the six-months list, then the five-years one, and finally the life list. Again, spend not more than one minute on each.

Once you have completed, this take a maximum of thirty seconds on each list to go back over your choices and verify that these are what you most want.

After doing the exercises, do you notice any patterns in your goals? How do the three lists compare? As you can imagine, the six-months list contains the things in life that are most important to you. If your life goals are fairly consistent with these, your direction in time is congruent. On the other hand, if your lifelong goals are very different from your six-months goals, you may want to take another look at your course in life.

CUSTOM-TAILORING YOUR USE OF TIME

Over the years as I have asked my seminar participants what they find most helpful in managing their time, the key shown in Figure 11.2 has emerged:

1. K^e—*physiology.* Make the best use of your best time. At what time of day are you most effective? Are you a morning person or a night person? When I get up at 4:30 or 5:00 A.M., if I work for an hour and a half right then and there, that time is probably equivalent to two and a half or three hours later in the day, because I am much more focused. If you aren't really awake until three in the afternoon, or if you are a night person, plan your day to make best use of your peak performance times.

   If you don't already know when you function best, monitor yourself for a few days to discover at what times of day you are most effective. The best use of your prime time is ideally for your most important and creative projects. It's also best if this time is uninterrupted.

   The other consideration regarding physiology is fatigue. If you experience fatigue, use principles in the last section of this chapter to reduce it or eliminate it entirely.

2. *Right-brain sensory planning.* A daily goal and activity list provides an external visual plan (V^e) as well as internally *seeing the whole picture** of how the day will unfold (V^i). This, of course, also engages the right side of the brain. Then as you go through the details of the day, it is easier to maintain perspective and balance. The writing itself is kinesthetic (K^e), and imagining how you will feel when your goals are accomplished gives an internal dimension (K^i). If you want an auditory dimension, you might talk to yourself as you make the list (A^e) and have that soft, soothing, sexy voice inside (A^i) invite you to enjoy the day's activities.

   The mistake many people make in daily planning is focusing

*Seeing the broader, whole picture is sometimes called *upchunking*—the opposite of downchunking, or breaking the whole into smaller parts.

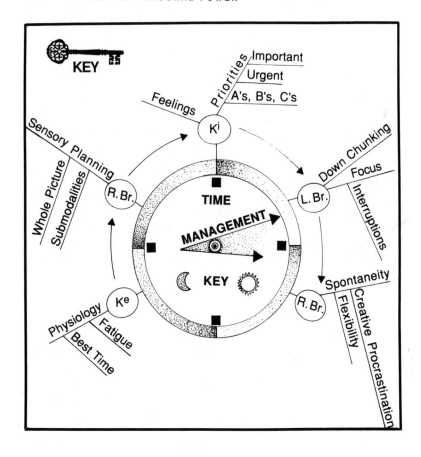

FIGURE 11.2

too much on the process or work of getting through the day, as opposed to imagining the outcomes. They often hear that internal scolding voice telling them what they have to do (A^i), feel the drudgery of the work ahead (K^i), and picture potential failure and missed deadlines. What gives power to daily planning is visualizing your success (V^i), hearing that inviting internal voice (A^i), and imagining how you will feel with your plans accomplished (K^i).

INSTEAD PICTURE SUCCESS AND FOCUS ON THE OUTCOME. KEEP RE-MINDING MYSELF - "BY DOING THIS, WHAT WILL MY OUTCOME BE."

A list also frees you from having to remember all the work projects, classes, assignments, errands, and social commitments you want to do that day. If you number your list according to priorities, you never have to worry about what to do next.

If you write your list on a 3″ by 5″ card or a folded piece of paper, you can keep it with you during the day. In that way you can enjoy the reward of crossing off items as you complete them. Also, it will be convenient to add new ideas for today or tomorrow as you think of them.

Some people like to make their list first thing in the morning, to start with freshness and clarity each day. Others prefer to plan the next day at the end of the afternoon or evening. They find it helps them let go of unfinished tasks and gives a greater continuity from one day to the next.

What works well for me is to do both—to note at the end of the day what I did and didn't get done, and what I would like to carry over to the next day. The next morning, with a fresh perspective, I review plans I made the evening before. Along with a daily list, weekly and monthly lists together with a pocket calendar allow a broader perspective. They help you see the larger picture of your life.

3. K^i—*feelings about the day's activities*. This step involves being honest with yourself in deciding how you feel about each planned activity or goal.

- Which items are you most inspired to do, and which do not overly excite you? In particular, decide the one item you least want to do, and make sure to do that item first. We will come back to this point in the section on reducing or eliminating fatigue.
- Distinguish between which items are *important* (positive K^i) vs. which are *urgent* (negative K^i). I wonder how many of us spend most of our time doing urgent things—meeting deadlines, working on crises, putting out fires. What about the *important* things? What's important is what you want to be doing over the course of your life and what is closest to your heart—your shortterm, midterm, and long-term goals. Are you doing something each day to move you closer to these goals?

URGENT DOES NOT NECESSARILY = IMPORTANT!

WHAT IS MY PAY-OFF? WHAT WILL I GET/GAIN?

Most experts on time management agree that it is essential to spend some time each day doing something to move closer to your goals, even if it is just a few minutes or half an hour. At least you will know you are making small steps and progress. Otherwise, if the only thing you are doing is meeting deadlines, and solving crises, what's the point?

• *Prioritize items on your list.* A classic system is A's, B's, and C's. The A's are top priority—you definitely want to do them today. These are items you cannot afford to postpone until tomorrow—an assignment at school, work due today or tomorrow, or progress toward your most important goals. The B's have second priority. It would be nice to do them today, but the world won't fall apart if you don't. The C's are of lower priority and do not require immediate attention. They are often small, easy jobs—shopping for shoes or picking up a *Consumer Reports* article on a car you may buy in a year.

After you start the day with that one item you least want to do, then do the A's first. In that way, if there are things you don't get to on your list, you have the most important things out of the way. In fact, I like to make three separate lists: the A's, the B's, and the C's. I almost always get all of the A's done, most of the B's, and maybe some of the C's. At the end of the day, instead of focusing on what I didn't do, I can see the most important things I accomplished and how I made the best use of my time.

You can ask yourself two questions that can help you prioritize: "What would happen if I didn't do this item today?" and "What's the worst that would happen if I didn't do this item at all?" Also, you want to make sure that your activity is bringing you some degree of personal happiness, growth, and satisfaction.

C MANIA

A common pitfall in time management is to get distracted from the difficult A's you are working on in favor of accomplishing a number of easier C's. In the midst of working on a report due tomorrow, you suddenly find yourself compelled to reorganize your closet, change your spark plugs, or call the Army buddy you haven't spoken with in fifteen years.

C's are often more appealing than A's because they are easier to do, more familiar, and run less risk of failure. If you feel you might be getting sucked into C's, ask yourself if the job you are doing really needs to be done now. "Do I really need to be alphabetizing my canned vegetables, or would it be better to be working on my income taxes, which have to be postmarked in two hours?" If you catch yourself absorbed in C's, be easy with yourself and gently bring yourself back to the more important tasks.

---

4. *Left-brain focus and downchunking.* One of the best ways to promote focus is to avoid interruptions. This is especially important during your prime time to help maintain focus and concentration. You might tell people around you that you work alone at certain hours—for example, between 8:00 A.M. and 10:30 A.M.—and will answer phone calls and get back to visitors later. An answering machine that screens calls can be a great help in this regard. You can leave a message stating the best times to reach you and ask your callers to leave a detailed message. Also, if you're expecting one important call, you can screen the others and get back to them later.

Of course, that's not always possible, so some people hide out during their prime time. Others come into work an hour or more early to get an undistracted start for the day and their important projects. With their increased efficiency they can often leave work earlier with more done.

Left-brain focus can also help you power through those least desirable or tedious projects you have a hard time getting started on. As with modular study, break the project into smaller pieces through downchunking (i.e., sessions of thirty to forty minutes). If it seems so dreadful you can't even muster the energy for this much time, work on it for just ten or fifteen minutes.

There is a principle from physics: *Static friction is greater than kinetic friction.* It is harder to get an object moving in the first place than to maintain motion once you get it moving.

You might decide at first not to work on the project but simply to spend ten to fifteen minutes to bring together the materials you will need to do it, or to find out how you can learn what you need to know to do it. The next day you might begin the project with the stipulation you will spend no more than fifteen minutes on it no matter how much you are enjoying it. After the project gets moving and you feel the relief of finally having it under way, you can allow yourself the treat of extending the chunks to longer periods of up to forty minutes each.

5. *Right-brain Spontaneity.*

- *Maintain a sense of flexibility.* Have in back of your mind the question "What is the best use of my time right now?" Maybe you had certain plans this morning, but a number of distractions and interruptions came up. Now it is forty-five minutes before your lunch break, so what would be the best use of your time? You might want to change your previous agenda.

  It's also a good idea to plan diversions during commutes and waiting times. Maybe you need to make a trip to the post office, and you know there is always a long line there. Reading a book while you stand in line is a marvelous way to improve the quality of your time. Likewise, travel and commuting times are excellent opportunities to learn a foreign language from cassette tapes. I'm learning several foreign languages during what might otherwise be dead time.

  If you have the kind of job where you have to sit around from time to time, bring some of your own projects to work with. With all of these methods, you'll find you're getting a lot more accomplished with your life.

- *Schedule "creative procrastination" time.* In her book *Creative*

Procrastination, Frieda Porat suggests leaving some of your time unscheduled. When scheduled tasks take longer than expected or interruptions occur, this allows leeway. If everything goes as planned, you have time for an extended break, a walk or a hike, or time to be spontaneous and do something you hadn't planned.

Scheduled time should have a limit—perhaps until late afternoon or dinner. Having some unstructured time each day puts a limit on the potential tyranny of left-brain orderliness and the right brain to be spontaneous. Unstructured time is also essential for artists, writers, and other creative people. It can be a time to let your heart lead you into deeply fulfilling activity.

There is a story of a wealthy farmer who lived in New England during Colonial times. His neighbors were a poor Indian family who also farmed. One day, out of a sense of compassion, the farmer offered to give the Indian family forty acres of his land. The Indian husband thanked the farmer for his generosity but turned him down, saying, "If I have all that extra land to work, when would I have time to sing?"

Knowing that your scheduled structured time has a limit is often a motivator to improve your efficiency during that time.

TIME LINES

Think for a second about your past. If you could imagine a physical direction for events in your past, which way would that be: toward your left? behind you? under you? Point in that direction. Next, think about your future. If you could visualize a direction for events in your future, which way would that be? Point in that direction. Finally, notice which way you might imagine events in the present: right in front of you? below you? maybe over to one side? Point in that direction. If you don't have a clear sense for these directions, give it your best guess.

TIME LINES (continued)

To sort events from the past, present, and future—that is, to distinguish which events go where—we all unconsciously assign various directions for different time periods. Connecting those directions together gives a straight line or sometimes a curve we call our time line.

A person who "lives in the past" may literally have a time line with the past more visible than with the present or the future. In the same way, someone who lives for tomorrow ("future-oriented") may have a time line with the future more visible than with the past or the present.

Therapies based on working with a person's time line have evolved to help people with time perception problems—someone who never learns from the past, or the person who lives only for now and can't plan for the future, or a person whose future appears dim. Time line work also provides techniques to make your dreams and goals more compelling.

PAPER FLOW

A golden rule for paper flow is to handle each piece of paper once or twice at most. If you do this, you will make immediate decisions, and stacks of unattended papers will no longer have the tyranny of tying up your mental energy.

Whatever mail I keep from my college mailbox goes into three stacks on my desk. The A stack—whatever is top priority and must be done today—is the only one that remains on my desk. The B stack would be nice to do today, but it isn't crucial. These items get filed into a pending bin or a tickler file to do later this week. The C items are papers and correspondence I can't quite throw away. Maybe one day I'll need them.

The classic remedy for C papers is a C drawer. I don't even take the time to file these items. If I ever need them, I can shuffle through the drawer and find them. Periodically I purge the drawer to see if the items are still of interest.

One last point on paper flow is use of your desk. Ideally, the desk is a tool for processing only current priority items for today. That's all you should see on the top of your desk.

REDUCING OR ELIMINATING FATIGUE

One of the biggest causes of fatigue is procrastination. Besides having to do an unpleasant task, looking forward to it may be unpleasant as well—a second source of fatigue. As we have discussed, a classic way to deal with procrastination involves putting that one item you least want to do first on your daily list. Follow this by the most important "A" items.

I wonder if you've ever done that and noticed how you feel afterward. Most people feel a sense of exhilaration knowing that the most difficult item for the day is done. It may not even be that important—apologizing to someone or signing some papers—but for whatever reason, you've been procrastinating. When you get that task over with, it frees up a lot of energy.

Be careful that the item you start with is not too big a project. Otherwise you might not do anything else that day. If it's too big, downchunk into small unpleasant pieces as we discussed earlier, and start with one chunk each day. At home I keep what I call my "procrastination list"—all the undone tasks from the past few months. I find that if I start the day with one of those items, as the list shrinks, my energy goes up. It's a direct relationship. Sometimes the easiest way to get started on a difficult project is simply to bring together all the materials you will need to do it.

Besides this, other things you can do to reduce or eliminate fatigue are:

• *Exercise.* Some of the best exercises for fatigue are also the best for cardiovascular fitness: aerobic exercise as recommended by the American Heart Association. Follow their guidelines: Exercise three to four times a week on alternate days. The exercise should get your pulse up to a certain level, depending on your age and physical condition. It should also be something you enjoy so you will keep up the routine. Dancing, hiking, cycling, aerobics, and swimming are all very stimulating.

A good, consistent routine will not only reduce your tendency toward fatigue, but you will also find increased clarity of thought and focus. Exercise makes you feel better—physically, mentally, and emotionally.

• *Diet.* The most crucial meal to eliminate fatigue is lunch. Two items to avoid for lunch are high-protein foods, and fats or oils.[1] The suggestion about protein may seem surprising, but most of us eat much more protein than our bodies can possibly use. What the body does not require, it breaks down, but at an energy drain to the body. The average American diet is also far richer than necessary in fats and sugar—an unhealthy way to get calories.

Your best bet for lunch is to go with complex carbohydrates and fresh fruits or vegetables. Complex carbohydrates include beans, corn, pasta, breads, potatoes, and rice—what we used to call starches. A complex carbohydrate is a complex sugar that breaks down slowly and supplies energy gradually over a long time. This is one of the major ways marathon runners get their energy.

If you eat raw fruits or raw vegetables, it is best not to have them both in the same meal. Raw fruits and raw vegetables require different digestive enzymes, which interfere with digestion of the other. If either is cooked, however, it doesn't matter.

If you follow the old maxim "Eat breakfast like a king, lunch like a prince, and dinner like a pauper," you will feel better and be less prone to fatigue. Also practice "systematic undereating."[2] Eat to a point that you are just about satisfied but could eat a little more—and stop. Too much digestive activity makes anyone sluggish.

Breakfast is a good time for high protein, since you have the rest of the day to digest it. For lunch it is best not to stuff yourself and to stay with the recommendations above. A light and early dinner improves the quality and depth of your sleep. Obviously, if your physician or nutritional counselor has given you other advice, follow it.

• *An afternoon nap or meditation break.* I'm not sure if you have a couch or a bed in your office, but a short afternoon nap can not only perk up the rest of the afternoon and evening but also may reduce the amount of sleep you require. Meditation is also an excellent way to eliminate fatigue and energize yourself.

- *Alternate physical and mental tasks and take breaks.* Varying tasks and routine can take some of the drudgery out of what you are doing. And as we've discussed, taking a break every thirty to forty minutes helps maintain energy and improves memory.
- *Periodic rewards:* These might include snacks, some time doing something you especially enjoy, or taking a walk; these can help motivate you to get through tedious tasks, and add richness to your passage through time.

CHAPTER TWELVE

*L*IVING LIFE WITH INTELLIGENCE AND PASSION

Ask yourself what you would do,
if you knew,
you could not fail
——ANTHONY ROBBINS

Intelligence is a measure of the overall performance of our brain. It is the basis of contemplating atoms, appreciating art, mastering sports, or feeling religious devotion. It is the foundation of enjoying what we see, hear, feel, smell, and taste. It is also basic to higher love and fulfilling our dreams.

Passion is the juice of being alive. It is the fire within our dreams, the spontaneity of now, the power behind empowering states, a key ingredient of true intelligence.

This chapter presents some innovative methods for improving intelligence and living with life with passion—through empowering states—for peak performance in learning, sports, and enjoyment of life.

INCREASING YOUR INTELLIGENCE

Intelligence as measured through IQ testing has been thought to peak when we reach adulthood (at about seventeen or eighteen). Beyond that age it was thought to remain fairly constant, and to decline with old age. People also believed that our IQ was mainly inherited.

As it turns out, environmental factors as we grow up can have profound effects on our intelligence. We can also improve our intelligence at any age with appropriate physical activity, mental exercises, and visualization.

Because a bit of well-directed practice with IQ-type questions can significantly improve the results, IQ testing has come under some criticism. In addition, IQ testing leaves out some qualities that could make a big difference in a person's overall intelligence, such as:

- flexibility and creativity
- independent thinking
- appreciation of beauty and humor
- originality in dealing with novel situations

There are, however, other forms of testing that take some of these factors into account.

SIX SECRETS TO IMPROVE YOUR INTELLIGENCE

Since intelligence enhances our appreciation and enjoyment of life, and since each of us *craves* greater achievement and happiness, I have chosen the acronym, CRAVES to illustrate six secrets to improving intelligence. These are.

- C: Circulation in your brain
- R: Right-brain/left-brain exercises
- A: Avoid dulling influences
- V: Visualization exercises

E: Enrich your environment

S: Synchronize your brain waves

FIGURE 12.1

Let's consider each of these.

1. *Circulation in your brain.* Improve the circulation in your brain. Some researchers have speculated that Einstein's genius was in part due to enhanced capillary circulation within his brain.

   As we have discussed earlier, after age thirty we lose brain cells at an average of roughly ten thousand per day. The 5 to 10 percent of your neurons that do develop to their full potential (thousands of dendrites) are presumably the best nourished; the ones that die off are likely the least nourished.

   Aerobic exercise, recommended by the American Heart Association, improves circulation and extension of the capillary system throughout the body—including, of course, the brain.

   In a Canadian study,[1] three hundred school-age children participated in an exercise program. As they became better fit physically, their grades simultaneously improved. Other studies have also demonstrated that exercise promotes better emotional stability, memory, and clearer thinking.

2. *Right-brain/left-brain exercises.* There is a growing body of evidence showing that by working to improve one area of the brain, other areas simultaneously improve. The two halves of the cortex are specialized but not isolated. Each side complements and improves the performance of the other. My suggestion to right-brain professionals such as artists, actors, dancers, and musicians is that they can improve their performance by taking a course in algebra, computers, or science. Left-brain professionals such as engineers, accountants, or clerical workers can improve their left-brain skills by taking a drawing class, a dance class, acting, or perhaps learning to play a musical instrument.

When school budgets are tight, what is the first thing to go? Art . . . music . . . drama—all right-brain activities! The potential here is that we are crippling our children intellectually. In a classic study[2] in Mead School in the Byram section of Greenwich, Connecticut, children spent 50 percent of their time doing traditional schoolwork and a full 50 percent of their time doing right-brain activities. Do you know what happened? Of course, the right-brain skills improved, but so did left-brain performance in areas such as math, science, and English grammar.

As we discussed earlier, drawing is a powerful means to put you in touch with right-brain functioning. Acting is another powerful approach. The other right-brain shifters discussed in Chapter Five are also useful.

There are a number of good books on logical puzzles that allow you to enhance left-brain functioning. Books designed to prepare you for IQ testing will also help. The left-brain shifters—crossword puzzles, making up puns, asking detailed questions—are useful. Good mystery books are another aid.

In planning your daily schedule, if you alternate mental and physical activity as well as right-brain and left-brain activities, you can improve your effectiveness.

3. *Avoid dulling influences.* Drug and alcohol abuse can not only distort your mental functioning but also literally kill or pickle millions of brain cells. Smoking affects your brain for the same reason it affects your heart: breathing in excess carbon monoxide. A single puff has ten to fifteen times the concentration of

carbon monoxide considered dangerous by air pollution author-
ities. Treat your brain with respect and dignity. Remember
that it is the most superb engineering feat we know of.

On the other side of the coin, you can promote sharp
functioning of your brain by taking care of your physiology—
with proper diet, exercise, and *proper rest*. Remember the
dietary strategies from Chapter Eleven to reduce fatigue and
increase energy.

see list

4. *Visualization exercises.* Improving your powers of visualization
will promote creativity, give you a clear internal picture of your
goals and success, and perhaps develop the corpus collosum
linking the left and right hemispheres. Dreams and images are
the language of the right. Interpreting and understanding these
images is a job for the left. The corpus collosum allows flow of
thought back and forth. Make use of the visual thinking
techniques from Chapter Five and the visual memory methods
from Chapter Seven.

5. *Enrich your environment* (and your children's). Numerous studies[3] on gifted children show that intelligence is not so much
hereditary as it is a result of a rich, stimulating environment,
especially during the first few years. Julius Caesar began his
schooling as a warrior riding into battle at age three with his
uncle. Alexander the Great also started quite young.

In the early 1800s a German doctor, Witte, set out to give his
son Karl completely enriched surroundings. Karl then entered
the University of Leipzig at age nine, and received his Ph.D. at
fourteen and his Doctorate of Law at sixteen.

Lord Kelvin, one of the great nineteenth-century physicists,
began with a rich early home environment. He was admitted to
the University of Glasgow at age ten and lived a full and
productive life to age eighty-three.

Mozart was immersed in his father's music and instruments
from birth. He was playing and composing by age five and
composed his first symphony at age eight.

In 1952 Aaron Stern[4] in New York gave his daughter an
enriched environment with classical music, flash cards with
numbers and pictures, and frequent talking to her with *no* baby
talk. By four she had read the *Encyclopaedia Britannica;* by
twelve she had entered college; and by fifteen she was teaching

higher mathematics at Michigan State University. Her IQ is about 200 (150 is considered genius level).

It is important to distinguish between providing a rich, stimulating environment as opposed to *pressuring* children to satisfy their parents' egos. The concept of early learning has come into question as a result of bad experiences children have had from excess parental pressure and the fear that early intellectual development will somehow detract from the child's emotional and social growth.

The fact is that when children grow up in an environment that is enriched, loving, and relaxed, they are not social misfits. They also don't tend to excel in only one field but do well in studies, artistic activities, leadership skills, and personal relationships. In one study,[5] Dr. Terman tested over a thousand people with an IQ over 135. He found their physical health to be better than the average population; their divorce rates were lower; and educational achievement was, of course, much better.

These results with children are well known. What has not been as well recognized is that adults might also benefit from enriched surroundings. Dr. J. Altman and Dr. Gopal Das[6] took a group of adults rats and set them up in a stimulating, enriched environment. The result after a few weeks was increased intelligence compared with the control group (biological relatives). Key areas of the brains of the rats in the enriched surroundings were observed to have improved dramatically in size and chemical functioning.

ACTIVITIES TO ENRICH YOUR ENVIRONMENT

- Try out new activities (things you've never done before).
- Take new courses of study.
- Cover all your senses when learning.
- Surround yourself with beauty, art, music, good lighting, and color.

ACTIVITIES TO ENRICH YOUR ENVIRONMENT
(continued)

- Vary your routine.
- Travel.
- Test your personal values and beliefs by trying out viewpoints that contradict your own.
- Have an appropriate balance of right-/and left-brain daily activities.
- Each day ask yourself, "What did I do today that was new and different?"

6. *Synchronize your brain waves.* One of the more powerful methods to enhance your intelligence and to put yourself into a resourceful state is also one of the simplest. It is an ancient mental-relaxation and stress-reduction technique that has recently been "rediscovered."

The brain puts out weak electrical signals called brain waves, or more technically EEG waves. These vary in frequency. Both sides of the brain put out a mixture of frequencies; the side more involved with the activity at hand puts out a stronger signal. The less-involved half puts out a weaker signal with more alpha waves, indicating it is more relaxed.

BRAIN WAVE TYPES

Type	Frequency	Associated with
Delta	0.5–4 Hz	Deep sleep
Theta	4–7 Hz	Deep meditation and reverie— "twilight" level of consciousness
Alpha	8–14 Hz	Relaxed state or daydreaming
Beta	14–22 Hz	Wakefulness; wide awake or engaged in mental activity

A common characteristic of the signals is that brain waves on one side are very different from brain waves on the other. This indicates that the two halves of the brain are not synchronized or coherent.

During practice of the mental relaxation technique mentioned above, something very different begins to occur. Dr. J. P. Banquet[7] observed that the brain waves become purified in frequency and synchronized between left and right. The waves are not identical but are much more alike than normal. After people practice this technique over a period of time, some of the brain waves synchrony begins to carry over into activity. This would seem to indicate more of a balanced functioning between left and right.

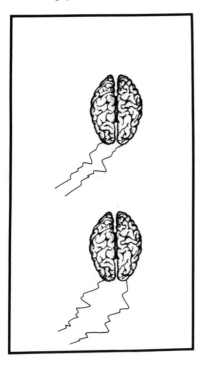

FIGURE 12.2

You might wonder what the advantage would be of sitting down, relaxing, and having your brain wave synchronized. Over six hundred scientific studies done on people experiencing this state of awareness have demonstrated some far-reaching benefits for memory, creativity, and intelligence.

Researchers have observed that when a person takes up this practice, both long-term and short-term memory immediately improved.[8] Comprehension and ability to focus also improve. Abstract reasoning (especially important in mathematics, sciences, and computers) improves, and creativity is enhanced.

Short-term studies have demonstrated an increase of intelligence as measured by field independence, and long-term studies[9] of three to five years show a steady increase of intelligence as measured by fluidity. This testing in contrast with usual IQ testing, is not altered by educational background or preparation. Later studies have shown a synchrony among the back, center, and front of the cortex, as well as vertical synchrony within the brain. Synchrony between the back and center of the cortex would suggest improved perceptual motor activities such as sports and dance. A number of studies have indeed shown this to be the case, and many professional athletes now practice this technique. Vertical synchrony may also account for autonomic changes such as in blood pressure, respiratory rate, and pulse observed to be considerably lower than in deep sleep.

At this point you are probably wondering what technique I am talking about. I've been describing a form of meditation called *Transcendental Meditation*, or TM for short. I am most familiar with this form of meditation, since I have practiced it for about twenty years. If you meditate fifteen or twenty minutes twice a day, you begin experiencing better memory, clearer thinking, increased physical well-being, synchronized brain waves, and empowering states more often.

Other forms of meditation may produce similar benefits, but TM is the most researched form and the only technique I am aware of that produces brain-wave synchrony to this extent. Transcendental meditation is taught one to one by trained teachers at TM centers in most larger cities throughout the world.

Now see if you can reconstruct the six secrets to increase your intelligence contained in CRAVES.

AGING AND MEDITATION[10]

Our biological aging can apparently be slowed as a result of meditation. Dr. Keith Wallace and others have discovered that people practicing TM for five to ten years frequently have a biological age five to ten years less than their actual age.

We have known for a long time that aging is very individual. It is as though we each have an internal biological clock, each running at a different rate. Now we may have a way to slow our clocks down.

POWER ANCHORS

Don and Dorris were celebrating their twentieth anniversary at a romantic restaurant with candlelight, champagne, inviting aromas, and soft music in the background. Don got up to request a certain song from the band, came back to the table, touched Dorris on the back of her neck in a certain way, and suddenly she felt depressed.

I wonder if you have had a similar experience of going through the day feeling fine, when suddenly, for no apparent reason, you are depressed . . . or maybe the reverse, where you are in a lousy mood when "something snaps" and you feel fine.

In Chapter Seven we discussed *memory anchors*, wherein a strong emotion or physical sensation becomes connected with or anchored to a memory. Beyond simple memories, a visual, auditory, or kinesthetic stimulus can trigger an emotion or an entire state. Such connections are called *state anchors*.

Do you notice feeling a sense of serenity when you look at your favorite painting? Perhaps "our song" brings back romantic feelings you had with that special someone. Or maybe you notice a different emotion when that stranger on the highway gives you an obscene gesture because you're not going ninety miles per hour. Each of these perceptions—the painting, the music, and the gesture—are neutral by themselves. Somewhere in the past our brains have linked or anchored these with states.

State anchors naturally occur when a V, A, or K experience becomes unconsciously linked with a memory or state. There was a time when children taking piano lessons would get their knuckles whacked with a ruler each time they made a mistake. No one could understand why so many people developed a fear of playing the piano.

I remember a time when I made it a point to call my old girlfriend at the end of a weekend of leading seminars. I was normally feeling satisfied at successfully completing the seminars and anxious to hear her voice, yet very tired. After some time I began to notice something strange: In the middle of a highly energetic day I could call her to chat and suddenly find myself feeling tired. I was beginning to wonder if the romance was waning when it occurred to me that I had inadvertently anchored the sound of her voice with feeling tired. Some psychologists in fact feel that the downfall of many romantic relationships is a mismatch of thinking styles (VAK) and too many negative anchors from unpleasant arguments, anger, and hurt that unconsciously become anchored with the other's face, tone of voice, or touch.

Positive-/and negative-state anchors are naturally created unconsciously. When stimulated or *fired* in the future, they elicit various states—some pleasant, some not so pleasant. Thus many states occur beyond our conscious awareness. Is it possible, however, to neutralize negative state anchors and create positive ones for the states we desire? The answer from NLP is a resounding "yes." The connection of a number of empowering states to a single stimulus is called a *power anchor*, and power anchors are likely the quickest and most powerful ways to access empowering and resourceful states.

Suppose, as an example, you wanted to create a state in which you feel powerful and confident. Or maybe you would like a state where you feel happy and joyful. Or perhaps your would like a state where you feel especially creative and flexible. In each case, proceed with the following steps:

CREATING A POWER ANCHOR

1. Find a quiet spot where you can sit comfortably undisturbed. Relax and breathe easily.
2. Go back to a time when you were totally experiencing your desired state. Be in that situation as if it were happening *now*. Notice the sights, sounds, and especially the feelings from that experience.
3. Intensify the feelings from this state. Finding and adjusting the submodalities that are most significant for you can be helpful here.
4. When the feelings reach a peak, do a *unique* stimulus: Touch some part of your body in an unusual way, speak an unusual word, or look at something unusual. The most crucial part of the entire process is having the stimulus coincide with the peak of the experience.

CREATING A POWER ANCHOR (continued)

5. Change your state by standing up, walking around, or drinking something for a few minutes.
6. Test the anchor by firing it—that is, experience the touch, sound, or sight. If you do not go back into the desired state, redo steps 2 to 6 or use a different stimulus for your anchor.
7. Whenever you naturally find yourself in the desired state, you can *stack* your anchor by firing it at the peak of that experience.
8. You can create a power anchor by stacking a number of different empowering states using the same anchor.

You can also create anchors for other people—touching your lover in a certain way when he or she is in a particularly resourceful state . . . stimulating your child at a magical moment of delight or discovery.

PEAK PERFORMANCE IN LEARNING

A crucial step toward owning the knowledge we wish to master is to be able to use it in a performance context—passing a test, using the new skills in a tennis match, being at one's best during a job interview. You may have used the reading, study, or memory techniques from this book to learn the material, so now you want to set up a state of peak performance for using it.

A natural starting point is to begin with your physiology—getting enough sleep the night before, imagining how you would be sitting or standing if you felt totally confident and empowered, and perhaps a few minutes of stretching or light exercise.

A powerful way to engage appropriate IR's is through a method called the George Technique. Dr. Donald Schuster from Iowa State University suggests the following, which should take five to ten minutes:

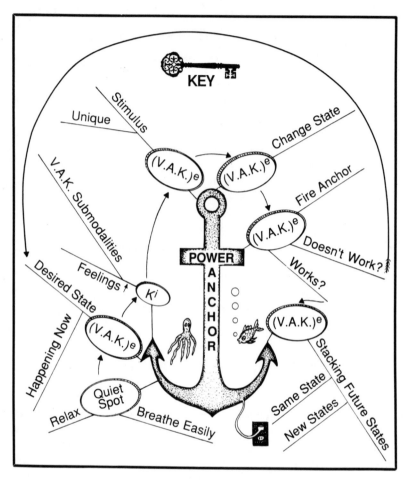

FIGURE 12.3

THE GEORGE TECHNIQUE[11]

The name George comes from an expression used in Colonial times. Whenever someone didn't want to do something or was procrastinating, the saying was "Let George do it."

The idea here is to give your unconscious a name: George, Georgette, or any other name to make this part of you more personal. Then when you have a stressful situation, such as a test, a job interview, a tennis match, or difficult learning, you can ask George or Georgette for help.

You can ask for help in two ways. One is to write a short note or letter: "Dear George (or Georgette): Here are the reasons why I would like to do well in this situation . . ." Then list the reasons. By doing this you are taking care of the left side of your brain with words, logic, linear thought, and reasoning.

For the right side of the brain, mentally project yourself into the activity. For example, if you are going to take a test, imagine yourself feeling confident and energetic. The adrenaline is starting to flow, and this leads you to peak performance. You are answering the questions, remembering everything, and working quickly. When test-taking in this easy state, what emotions do you feel? What do you feel in your body? How do things look? How do they sound? Finally, thank that unconscious part of you as if you had already succeeded.

You cover the left brain with the note and the right brain with the mental imagery. The sense of gratitude is also important. The more thankful you are for the help your unconscious provides, the more it wants to help in the future. In a very real sense, you are establishing the link between your own conscious and unconscious minds.

VISUALIZE

The last and most powerful step in establishing your state is to fire your power anchor. In fact, if you are pressed for time, it is enough just to do the steps for your physiology and use the anchor. If time allows, add the George Technique.

If your performance situation is a test, here are a few more suggestions:

- *Anchor success to the physical setting where you will be taking the test*. If possible, take some practice questions that you feel confident about into the same room where you will be taking the test. Gain the experience of successfully answering testlike questions in that setting. If that room is not available, see if you can find a nearby room that is reasonably similar in layout and setting.
- *Gain right-brain perspective and elicit unconscious help*. Read the test questions through before starting to work so you can begin to see the whole picture. Start on easier questions to begin the momentum of success. When you get stuck on a question, mark it, and return to it later. This allows your unconscious to work on the problem while you are successfully working on other questions.
- *Construct pattern discovery maps to help answer essay questions*. This is the quickest way to see the whole picture of how to organize your thoughts. The map also facilitates pulling missing chunks from memory.
- *In the event of test anxiety or panic, look up*. The problem with taking a test and experiencing anxiety is that you are looking down to answer the questions. This kinesthetic pose perpetuates more unpleasant feelings. To reduce or eliminate these feelings, change your physiology. Take a few minutes to assume a visual posture—sitting straight up and looking up. It is very difficult to maintain unpleasant feelings in this position. Beyond that you might briefly stretch or sharpen your pencil.

SIX SUCCESS SECRETS

The ultimate formula to achieve the success you want and deserve consists of six little secrets—SMARTS:

S: Specific goals
M: Motivation
A. Act
R: Reward system
T: Think clearly and powerfully
S: Stay with it

Let's see how each of these influences your success in learning, improving your relationships, changing your habits, or advancing your career.

1. *Specific goals*. Many failures in life come from lack of clear, specific goals. You need to know clearly the outcome you desire. If you get on an airplane and just start flying without a specific destination, you are liable to wind up anywhere. Even if you go to a travel agency and say you want to go to Hawaii, they can't help you. Hawaii is too nonspecific. Where in Hawaii? However, if you say you want to go to Honolulu on March 20, now you are getting somewhere.

   Once you have a specific goal of *what you want, by what date*, the next step is to answer the following questions: How will you know when you have achieved your goal? What evidence is required? If, for example, you desire to be wealthy, how much money will it take before you consider yourself wealthy? If you want more happiness, what evidence will you use to decide you are happy?

   With this specific information your unconscious can program you mentally to allow you to achieve that goal. Be specific and detailed in the results you want—not how you are going to achieve those results. The unconscious mind will generate creative ideas and plans you never dreamed of. Then you will become open to those occurrences and circumstances in daily life that will support your success. All you need is to know clearly what you want and how you will know when you have achieved it.

   Choosing models whose success you would like to develop also helps. You might also write out your goals and post them in a conspicuous place as a daily reminder of your life's direction.

2. *Motivation*. It is essential that you cultivate desire and interest in your goal, whether it is getting an "A" in a computer class or getting twenty consecutive tennis serves in. The more motivated you are, the easier it is to learn to remember and to advance your skills.

   The two most powerful ways to cultivate motivation are to use your motivation key and your power anchor. In addition, visualizing your success with the George Technique enables

Specific Goals: Know your outcome and how you'll know when you have achieved it. It's not enough to want to improve your tennis serve. Better would be, "I'd like to be able to hit 20 consecutive serves within 3 feet of the service box corners."

FIGURE 12.4

your right brain to see the whole picture of achieving success, and your left brain to sort through details of the step-by-step sequence of events necessary to reach your goal.

You can also enhance motivation by adopting some of the beliefs of people you model. Of course, you only want to use those beliefs that will contribute to what you want to achieve. For example, I would love to have the skills and strategies of certain tennis stars, but could certainly do without their manners on the court.

EXERCISE 33: UNCONSCIOUS SUPPORT

One of the most crucial factors for effective motivation is to have 100 percent support from your unconscious. If part or parts of you are ambivalent about the goal, you are likely to self-sabotage your efforts. A powerful way to check for unconscious support and to resolve discrepancies is to answer and/or resolve certain questions about your goal honestly.

As an example, pick one specific goal and honestly answer and/or resolve these three key questions:

5. What positive benefits do you now have as a result of not having your goal?
6. Is there a way you can achieve your goal without having to give up these positive benefits? How can you do this?
7. Can you think of specific circumstances in which you would be better off without your goal? How can you resolve this?

Answering these questions may bring to the surface limiting beliefs that have been holding you back. It is important to examine the merits of these beliefs, how they may once have served you, and if you may now want to change some of them.

TRY A CLUSTER OR MIND MAP

Setting specific goals makes your dreams concrete. Motivation fuels those dreams.

3. *Act.* Get yourself moving. Physics tells us that it is harder to get something moving than to keep it moving once it has started. Act without too much planning. Just get started.

A crucial first step toward action and change is to *accept yourself as you are now.* Only then do you have a clear reference point for change. Faith and self-trust are crucial to establish positive motivation and to undo your past negative beliefs or "learning blocks."

To build positive beliefs, concentrate your attention on your strengths, and acknowledge your successes as they occur.

Gratitude toward your unconscious mind is important here. The more you acknowledge your unconscious for its help, the more it is likely to help in the future.

4. *Reward system.* Set up a system of rewards or treats for achieving steps along the way for both short-term and long-term goals. This is a concrete way of expressing gratitude for the help your unconscious gives. Take time out for a movie, a picnic, a concert, or just free time to do nothing. Unstructured time can provide you with some of your most creative ideas.

Many people use rewards, but make the mistake of treating themselves well too infrequently. Some education specialists suggest at least once or twice per week. I agree.

Suppose you want to establish the habit of studying Spanish forty-five minutes each day. Psychologists tell us that it takes about twenty-one days to establish a daily routine as a habit.[13] To set up a reward system, divide twenty-one days into seven intervals of three days each. Then give yourself a gift or a treat at the end of each segment. Almost anyone can do an activity for just three days, and you'll be surprised at how quickly study becomes an automatic part of your routine. Using techniques in this book, you could learn about twenty-five hundred words and be conversationally fluent in Spanish or any other foreign language within about six months.

5. *Think clearly and powerfully.* Clear thinking and decision making can be clouded by strong emotions, including fear. The right-brain/left-brain shifters from Chapter Five allow you to shift easily away from any emotions that cloud movement toward your goals. Use visual, auditory, and kinesthetic thinking for appropriate situations.

Thinking powerfully also involves sensory acuity. Is what you are doing getting you the results you want? If not, take a different approach.

6. *Stay with it.* Specific goals start you moving, motivation fuels the process, but *persistence* and *flexibility* are what keep you on the path. Most people are too easily discouraged by what they perceive as failures. Consider this: Thomas Edison had nearly ten thousand failures before his first successful light bulb. Apparently he didn't even think of his first ten thousand tries as failures. Each one taught him how *not* to build a workable bulb.

HOW BEST TO USE POWERLEARNING

Powerlearning is in fact a philosophy of gaining personal power through enhanced memory, learning, thinking, and a collection of techniques. The methods are helpful only to the extent that we make good use of them. I suggest to my seminar participants that they are most likely to be successful if they implement the methods a little at a time.

Start with a few simple techniques in those areas of life that are most pressing, whether that be improving your reading skills, discovering and using your motivation key, improving your memory, managing your time and energy, or setting up a power anchor for yourself.

The uniqueness of Powerlearning is that we can experience the states we desire in dreams fulfilled as a means to achieve those dreams.

The value of improving your learning skills through Powerlearning is this: No matter what your goals, dreams, and desired states in life, achieving them always involves learning. To the extent that you can remember, think, and learn more effectively, you own your personal power—the ability and the choice to create what you desire.

Reading Pretest

FOR CHAPTER EIGHT

Record your starting time in hours, minutes, and seconds. To make things easier, wait for an even starting time such as: Hrs. 4 Min. 05 Sec. 00. As soon as you have finished, record the end time and subtract to get the actual reading time. Later you will find a chart to get your reading speed. As soon as you are ready, record your starting time and begin.

	Hours	Minutes	Seconds
End time	⎯⎯	⎯⎯	⎯⎯
Starting time	⎯⎯	⎯⎯	⎯⎯
Reading time	⎯⎯	⎯⎯	⎯⎯

"From Plankton to Whales" from Kon-Tiki by Thor Heyerdahl.[1]

It is certain that there must be very nourishing food in these almost invisible plankton which drift about with the current on the oceans in infinite numbers. Fish and sea birds which do not eat plankton themselves live on other fish or sea animals which do, no matter how large they themselves may be. Plankton is a general name for thousands of species of visible and invisible small organisms which drift about near the surface of the sea. Some are plants (phyto-plankton), while others are loose fish ova and tiny living creatures (zoo-plankton). Animal plankton live on vegetable plankton, and

58

54

112

vegetable plankton live on ammonia, nitrates, and nitrites which are formed from dead animal plankton. And while they reciprocally live on one another, they all form food for everything which moves in and over the sea. What they cannot offer in size they can offer in numbers.

In good plankton waters there are thousands in a glassful. More than once persons have starved to death at sea because they did not find fish large enough to be spitted, netted, or hooked. In such cases it has often happened that they have literally been sailing in strongly diluted, raw fish soup. If, in addition to hooks and nets, they had had a utensil for straining the soup they were sitting in, they would have found a nourishing meal—plankton. Some day in the future, perhaps, men will think of harvesting plankton from the sea to the same extent as they now harvest grain on land. A single grain is of no use, either, but in large quantities it becomes food.

The marine biologist, Dr. A. D. Bajkov, told us of plankton and sent us a fishing net which was suited to the creatures we were to catch. The "net" was a silk net with almost three thousand meshes per square inch. It was sewn in the shape of a funnel with a circular mouth behind an iron ring, eighteen inches across, and was towed behind the raft. Just as in other kinds of fishing, the catch varied with time and place. Catches diminished as the sea grew warmer farther west, and we got best results at night, because many species seemed to go deeper down into the water when the sun was shining.

If we had no other way of whiling away time on board the raft, there would have been entertainment enough lying with our noses in the plankton net. Not for the sake of the smell, for that was bad. Nor because the sight was appetizing, for it looked a horrible mess. But because, if we spread the plankton out on board and examined each of the little creatures separately with the naked eye, we had before us fantastic shapes and colors in unending variety.

Most of them were in tiny shrimp like crustaceans (copepods) or fish ova floating loose, but there were also larvae of fish and shellfish, curious miniature crabs in all colors, jellyfish, and an endless variety of small creatures which might have been taken from Walt Disney's *Fantasia*. Some looked like fringed, fluttering spooks cut out of cellophane paper, while others resembled tiny red-beaked birds with hard shells instead of feathers. There was no end to Nature's extravagant inventions in the plankton world; a surrealistic artist might well own himself here.

Where the cold Humboldt Current turned west south of the equator, we could pour several pounds of plankton porridge out of the bag every few hours. The plankton lay packed together like cake in colored layers—brown, red, gray and green according to the different fields of plankton through which we had passed. At night, when there was phosphorescence about, it was like hauling a bag of sparkling jewels. But, when we got hold of it, the pirates' treasure turned into millions of tiny glittering shrimps and phosphorescent fish larvae that glowed in the dark like a heap of live coals. When we poured them into a bucket, the squashy mess ran out like a magic gruel composed of glowworms. Our night's catch looked as nasty at close quarters as it had been pretty at a long range. And, bad as it smelled, it tasted correspondingly good if one just plucked up courage and put a spoonful of it into one's mouth. If this consisted of many dwarf shrimps, it tasted like shrimp paste, lobster, or crab. If it was mostly deep-sea fish ova, it tasted like caviar and now and then like oysters.

The inedible vegetable plankton were either too small that they washed away with the water through the meshes of the net, or they were so large that we could pick them up with our fingers. "Snags" in the dish were single jellylike coelenterates like glass balloons and jellyfish about half an inch long. These were bitter and had to be thrown away. Otherwise everything could be eaten, either as it was or cooked in fresh water as gruel or soup. Tastes differ. Two men on board thought plankton tasted delicious, two thought they were quite good, and for two the sight of them was more than enough. From a nutrition standpoint they stand on a level with the larger shellfish, and, spiced and properly prepared, they can certainly be a first class dish for all who like marine food.

That these small organisms contain calories enough have been proved by the blue whale, which is the largest animal in the world and yet lives on plankton. Our own method of capture, with the little net which was often chewed up by hungry fish, seemed to us sadly primitive when we sat on the raft and saw a passing whale send up cascades of water as it simply filtered plankton through its celluloid beard. And one day we lost the whole net in the sea.

"Why don't you plankton-eaters do like him?" Torstein and Bengt said contemptuously to the rest of us, pointing to a blowing whale. "Just fill your mouths and blow the water out through your mustaches!"

I have seen whales in the distance from boats, and I have seen them stuffed in museums, but I have never felt toward the gigantic carcass as one usually feels toward proper warm-blooded animals, for example a horse or an elephant. Biologically, indeed, I had accepted the whale as a genuine mammal, but in its essence it was to all intents and purposes a large cold fish. We had a different impression when the great whales came rushing toward us, close to the side of the raft.

One day, when we were sitting as usual on the edge of the raft having a meal, so close to the water that we had only to lean back to wash out our mugs, we started when suddenly something behind us blew hard like a swimming horse and a big whale came up and stared at us, so close that we saw a shine like a polished shoe down through its blowhole. It was so unusual to hear real breathing out at sea, where all living creatures wriggle silently about without lungs and quiver their gills, that we really had a warm family feeling for our old distant cousin the whale, who like us had had not even the sense to stick up its nose for a breath of fresh air, here we had a visit from something which recalled a well-fed jovial hippopotamus in a zoological gardens and which actually breathed—that made a most pleasant impression on me—before it sank into the sea again and disappeared.

Now record your ending time and answer the following questions *before* computing your reading time and speed. Do not look back at the reading section to answer these. Pick the best answer for each question.[2]

1. Individual plankton are invisible.
   (T) True; (F) False
2. The net with which the author caught plankton was a funnel of fine silk, almost 300 meshes per square inch.
   (T) True; (F) False
3. Plankton seems to be more plentiful in colder waters.
   (T) True; (F) False
4. Not all plankton are edible.
   (T) True; (F) False
5. The definition of plankton that emerges from the article is
   a. strongly diluted, strongly smelling, brilliantly colored fish soup
   b. the basic food for every creature that moves in or over the sea

    c. a general name for thousands of species of minute organisms, both vegetable and animal, that drift near the surface of the sea

X d. tiny animals that live in the sea, mostly fish ova, larva, and shrimp, with an occasional jellyfish

    e. whale food

6. Plankton may be important in the future, the author suggests, because

    a. it can save the lives of castaways at sea

    b. it provides the basic food for edible fish in commercially important quantities

X c. we may learn to harvest it

    d. its presence or absence provides a map of the currents of the ocean

    e. none of the above is correct

7. Which of the following was *not* a characteristic of plankton?

    a. phosphorescence

    b. great variety of forms and colors

    c. a foul smell

X d. uniformity of flavor

    e. delicious flavor once you got up the nerve to try it

8. To the author, the most memorable feature of the whale they sighted was

    a. its size

    b. its blowhole, shiny as a polished shoe

X c. its breathing

    d. its jovial, harmless disposition

    e. its sudden, silent disappearance into the sea

9. To the reader, the most remarkable feature of the story of the encounter with the whale is

    a. the danger the raft was in

    b. the surprising safety of the raft

X c. the contrast between the danger the reader can imagine, and the light, matter-of-fact way in which the story is told

    d. the way the whale's "personality" is rapidly sketched

    e. the offhand bravery of the members of the expedition

10. The logical connection between plankton and whales, which explains why the author discusses them together in this passage, is

    a. the fact that humans will learn to strain plankton out of the sea for food, as whales have always done

    b. the fact that both whales and plankton are marine animals

   c. the contrast between the smallest marine life and the largest
 ✗ d. the fact that whales, the largest of marine life, depend for food
      completely on plankton, the smallest
   e. the fact that the whale appeared immediately after the men's
      first appearance with the plankton

Now to get your reading speed in minutes and seconds as well as in
words per minute (wpm), consult the following table:

min.:sec.	1:30	1:40	1:50	2:00	2:10	
wpm	823	738	671	615	568	

min.:sec.	2:20	2:30	2:40	2:50	3:00	3:10
wpm	527	492	461	434	410	388

min.:sec.	3:20	3:30	3:40	3:50	4:00	4:10
wpm	369	351	335	321	308	295

min.:sec.	4:20	4:30	4:40	4:50	5:00	5:20
wpm	284	273	263	254	246	231

min.:sec.	5:40	6:00	6:20	6:40	7:00	7:30
wpm	217	205	194	185	176	164

min.:sec.	8:00	8:30
wpm	154	145

Record your speed on this page or on a separate piece of paper.
Answers to the questions follow. If you missed one, your comprehension is 90 percent; two, 80 percent;, etc.

Your speed ____ wpm. *136*
Your comprehension is ____ percent. *60%*

Answer key:

Question:	1	2	3	4	5	6	7	8	9	10
Answer:	F	F	F	T	T	c	c	d	c	c

Keep your results in a safe place to compare with a later test after you
have practiced some reading techniques and exercises.

*Y*OUR SIXTY DAY

READING PROGRAM

If you want to reach the highest reading speed available to most humans, take about ten to twenty minutes per day on the following set of exercises and suggestions. Make sure you have read Chapter Nine before starting this program, since these suggestions are based on the key presented there.

Keep track of your reading speed on the progress chart that follows the exercises. To compute your reading speed in words per minute (wpm), count the number of words on an average page. Read a number of pages and time yourself.

$$\text{wpm (speed)} = \frac{\text{number of pages read x number of words per average page}}{\text{number of minutes reading}}$$

By doing these exercises, you should be able to double and possibly triple your reading speed within sixty days. Comprehension should also improve significantly.

1. K^e—*physiology.* Whenever you read, practice:

- holding the material for an upright visual posture; if the book is heavy, support the weight on the front edge of your table or desk, or get a book holder
- use a visual aid (a pencil)

You can further improve the kinesthetic quality of reading through:

- *Metronome training.* If you have access to a metronome used for timing music, you can use it to establish and maintain a smooth, consistent reading rhythm. Set the metronome at a comfortable speed. Then let each tick correspond to one line with your visual aid. In this way you can avoid the slowdown that normally occurs after reading for a while.

Knowing the tempo allows you to know your reading rate. Over the sixty days you can gradually increase the tempo to push your speed ahead.

2. Right brain—*involve the right brain more through prereading.*

- For nontechnical or lighter reading, preread the first one or two sentences of each paragraph in the reading section or assignment except introductions, summaries, and conclusions, which you read thoroughly.
- For difficult or technical reading, read everything the first time through without regard to understanding.

3. V^e—*optimize the quality of visual input.* Do this through the following exercises:

A. *Eye swing warm-up (two minutes a day).*[1] The exercise that follows will help you improve the mechanics of moving your eyes across the page. It works primarily to reduce the number of stops your eyes make on each line of print, and to smooth out the rhythm of those stops. At the same time, if your reading habits include any eye movement uncertainty when returning from the end of one line to the beginning of the next, this exercise will help you eliminate that problem.

"Read" these pages by glancing very briefly at each bar, moving from left to right along each line. Work very quickly, or without being aware of it you will make more stops than the bars indicate. Be especially careful to make a fast return sweep from the end of one line to the beginning of the next.

Until you have tried it on several occasions, you probably will not feel that the exercise is comfortable. However, one "reading" is enough on any occasion. Practice this exercise just before reading each speed exercise in this manual.

Of course, in normal reading the stops you make on the line are determined partly by the phrases read, which may not be spaced as evenly as the bars here.

B. *High-speed practice.* Spend ten minutes per day reading much faster than your normal reading rate. Use any light material of your choice, preferably something of interest to you. Try for as much comprehension as possible, but know that this practice is primarily about speed.

C. *Shortening the lines by one-half inch.* Practice this technique, as explained in Chapter Nine.

D. *Phrase-flashing warm-up (3 minutes a day).*[2] This exercise expands your eye focus from the usual average of 1.1 words per fixation to the optimum level of 2.5 words with each stop. You don't necessarily take in a whole phrase per stop while reading normal text, but these exercises will broaden your peripheral vision.

The object of this exercise is to expand your eye focus. The phrases in the following material start short and get progressively longer. The object is to look at each phrase for the briefest possible fraction of a second, so you must read it in one glance. Start with Group A. When you can complete it without difficulty, go on to Group B, and so on.

With a sheet of paper, cover the columns you are not working with. Also, cover the column you are using with a 3" by 5" card. Move the card down to expose the first phrase and then back up again with the quickest possible flick of the wrist, so the first phrase in the column is exposed for an instant. Then tell yourself what you saw. If you are certain, guess, and then check yourself. Now do the same for the second word in the column, and so forth on down the column.

Group A

iconoclastic	a success story	the coal miners
on this spot	more and more	her purple dress
out on strike	get out of hand	strange question
beat them all	the grim reaper	It's not worth it.
ignorant of it	savage repartee	in the same boat
at high speed	once and for all	student rebellion
miss the boat	the other media	old acquaintance
came too late	bright and early	musical evenings
a key witness	being in fashion	lead him a dance
money orders	ulterior motives	He's impractical.
vital statistics	five months ago	not my fair share
thunderstruck	notwithstanding	source of income
the spare tires	before and after	far from accurate
along that line	better than ever	do the impossible
afraid to think	What time is it?	unusual endeavor
as they do say	in the meantime	graduate students
bacteriological	free information	an optical illusion
vegetable crop	finished product	whiskey and soda
our way of life	beyond question	They don't know.
old comic strip	He had seen me.	as clear as crystal

Group B

under suspicion?	The sky is clear.	take another look?
bigger and better	be that as it may	in the final analysis
largest molecules	get along without	acts like a chimney
I don't believe it.	as a matter of fact	a million and a half
basic significance	of real importance	relative instabilities
legal professional	the Panama Canal	world trouble spots
in the first quarter	it stands to reason	fencing instructions
incomprehensible	almost as much as	Start all over again.
no brighter future	from bad to worse	good administration
a perfect example	freedom of speech	molecular biologists
for the time being	a new lease on life	over and over again
so greatly in need	under construction	We are not amused.
the political scene	staggering problem	5 barrels of gasoline
a patent absurdity	extremely valuable	crude oil production
a flying laboratory	a standard practice	at your convenience
Council of Europe	inferiority complex	few and far between
the primary lesson	another application	at this time last year
bone of contention	a college education	a sharp straight nose
balance the budget	Second World War	will not be permitted
turn back the clock	theory and practice	to settle the question

Group C

effective operations
crude oil drilling rig
dissatisfied customer
partly for this reason
Take my word for it.
perfunctory applause
What a brilliant idea!
to explain these facts
manipulate the media
precision instruments
vote of no confidence
to add insult to injury
it now seems possible
It's too much trouble.
setting out poinsettias
unpolluted waterways
Estimate your results.
no fluorescent lighting
coal and iron reserves
psychological moment
He said nothing at all.
by the end of the year
change in temperature
three remarkable facts
the nineteenth century
of all the requirements
He bets on the horses.
It goes without saying.
unhappily disorganized
the local representative

Is he a reliable man?
millions of Europeans
based upon experience
How much did it cost?
devastating earthquake
produce the best result
overwhelming majority
throughout the country
a necessary adjustment
to play into their hands
It's not very important.
important contributions
make enough to live on
circumstantial evidence
It's a matter of custom.
a presidential candidate
because of bad weather
if the truth were known
throughout the universe
a serious miscalculation
big electrical appliances
in what has gone before
a problem of nationality
He rose from the ranks.
How fast can you read?
a reciprocal relationship
you simply can't impose
Roman Catholic Church
three different languages
You know what I mean.

Group D

first virus crystallized
a dramatic monologue
we lack the incentives
training and experience
this anarchistic outlook
What splendid animals!
an awkward disposition
the humanistic tradition
I shall be most grateful.
our analysis has implied
That accusation is false.
a rapid circulation of air
really needs overhauling
a personal responsibility
in international relations
under the circumstances
that you follow this plan
They can easily be seen.
a functional arrangement
great financial difficulties
take it into consideration
attorneys for the defense
no foreign correspondent
Supreme Court decisions
no mechanical difficulties
engineering achievements
noncommissioned officers
eighteenth-century novels
House of Representatives
United Nations Assembly

running around in circles
happily playing the piano
try to discover new ways
when all is said and done
it brings in the whole line
at the end of four months
This need not prevent us.
many years of experience
started moving cautiously
due to prior commitments
for some special comment
We have great confidence.
bewildered and withdrawn
the Union of South Africa
The verdict was "Guilty."
in three different countries
underground storage tanks
The whole thing is absurd.
many-branched candelabra
we may approach the work
an alternative interpretation
no hospitalization insurance
a Constitutional amendment
two political representatives
Governor of South Carolina
about the fifteenth of March
three wars in one generation
Mutual Broadcasting System
We may have made an error.
resume the military operation

4. A^i—*eliminate subvocalizing for nontechnical or lighter reading.* Practice these suggestion from Chapter Nine:

   • knuckle biting; or
   • number mumbling; or
   • high-speed practice.

5. A^i—*use subvocalizing for difficult or technical reading.* Have the voice inside be questioning, anticipating, and actively involved.

6. K^i—*learn to derive more pleasure from reading.* This should be a natural outcome of using this key to improve your speed and comprehension.

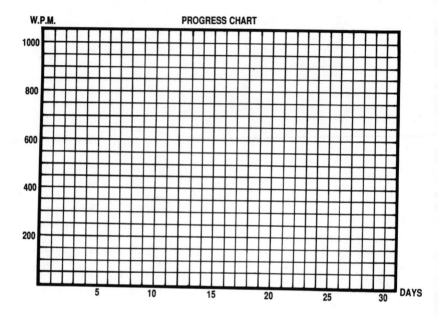

READING AFTERTEST FOR CHAPTER EIGHT

As before, you will read an article, time your reading speed, and answer some questions to check your comprehension. Be sure to use a pencil as a visual aid. The text is structured with vertical lines for "shortening the lines." Keep the visual aid between these two lines. Also, incorporate the prereading. Read only the first one or two sentences the first time through, then go back and read everything. Include both readings in your reading time.*

Record your reading time in hours, minutes, and seconds, as before. As soon as you are finished, record the end time. A table following the articles will again give your reading speed.

As soon as you are ready, record your starting time and begin.

	Hours	Minutes	Seconds
End time	____	____	____
Starting time	____	____	____
Reading time	____	____	____

*Sometimes including the prereading will result in an initial slowdown of your overall reading speed. With practice, most people can do both readings faster than a single reading before. The big advantage from prereading is increased focus and comprehension.

SURPRISING Rx FOR A RICHER, HAPPIER LIFE[1]

- Greg Haber, a college dropout, tried the Army as a career, but after four years realized it was not for him. He finally began to find himself as a real-estate salesman. But there were problems: depression, headaches, and heart palpitations that defied medical diagnosis.

  Today Greg, age forty-five, is free of his aliments. The wonder drug, he reports, is education. On a psychologist's recommendation, he enrolled in a weekend college course unrelated to his job that proved to be the only medicine he needed.

- Robertson Beck was suffering from a nervous breakdown, compounded by the loss of his job and the breakup of his marriage. His excuse for his failures was that he has had to abandon a promising architectural career because of his financial problems. "Go back to your studies," a family counselor advised the thirty-nine-year-old Beck. "Support your education with any part-time work you can get, but study as though your life depended on it—as indeed it may."

  Beck did just that. Today he has a degree and a new career. But he is continuing to take courses because they "sharpen my ability to concentrate and improve the mental stamina I need in my job."

- Emily and Ralph Peters, a middle-aged couple, were "bored to oblivion" by a calisthenics class. "Exercise is a bust when it becomes routine," explained Ralph, "so we salvaged our sanity by enrolling in something different—a course in archaeology. Every week we hike and climb and do various kinds of manual labor on field trips—more exercise than we ever got on that smelly gym floor. Our brains get exercise, too, so we end up feeling mentally fit as well as physically fit."

Adult education has long been on the upsweep, with millions of Americans of all ages going back to school—in the evenings, on weekends, while on leave of absence from a job, even during holidays and vacations. Yet only recently has there been evidence of correlations among continuing education, mental well-being, physical health, and, in some cases, even longevity.

Dr. Robert Samp, a physician and health educator at the University of Wisconsin Medical School, has for many years conducted research on why some people live longer than others. He discovered what he terms "a protective intuition" in old people whose lives remain meaningful. Based on his studies of more than two thousand older Americans, Dr. Samp says, "There is plenty of indication that taking courses is a beneficial activity, contributing to good health."

Dr. John B. Moses of Scarsdale, New York, a physician with long experience in the field of aging (among the young and middle-aged as well as the old), says, "Activity slows down the aging and hardening process in blood vessels. You may not think of learning as something 'active.' But it involves the entire body, including vision, hearing, other senses, motor activity, reflexes, and, of course, that mysterious attribute we call motivation. To me, the learning process and its demands all add up to a healthier existence—at any age."

The Academy for Educational Development (AED), a non-profit planning and research organization, has conducted hundreds of interviews with people in their sixties and older who have returned to the classroom. Typical reactions: "It's the surest way to keep my mind active." "The classroom is the best medicine there is for an adult who wants to stay healthy and enjoy life." "These courses have made a new woman out of me."

"Education is a means for individuals to adapt to accelerated change," says psychologist James E. Birren, director of the Ethel Percy Andrus Gerontology Center at the University of Southern California. "Thus, continuing education over the life span is not only desirable; it may become essential."

Education is like exercise. You can improve your health by starting an exercise program after you retire, even if you never have done so. But you are obviously better off if you are continuing a program you started earlier.

Robert Adamson, director of the College at Sixty program at Fordham University's Lincoln Center campus in New York City, reports that older students likely to benefit most from structured college education "are those who have enjoyed learning all along. They have the healthiest mental outlook."

"Any program of study—formal or casual—that gets participants involved and motivated is likely to be beneficial," says Alvin C. Eurich, president of AED. "The most valuable programs, though, are those that continue over the years and develop lifetime learning habits."

William Berkeley is president of Elderhostel, a successful program of one- and two-week courses on college campuses for people sixty years of age and older. "You cannot imagine," he told me, "what a 'wonder drug' it is for older people to discover that not only can they cope with classroom demands, but many of them can perform as successfully as the other, younger students in their regular classroom sessions. Morale skyrockets; they see better, hear better, feel better. Education is the most effective tonic they could find."

This doesn't mean everyone must sign up for courses in adult education programs. Structured curricula are the most feasible for many because they offer specific sequences of study, cultivate regularity of activity, and often provide some form of evaluation. Yet the "mental jogger" who prefers to pursue education by himself can achieve the same benefits, if properly motivated.

The exact relationship between education and health may never be proved scientifically—there are too many additional factors. But evidence of learning's positive effects continues to mount. And meanwhile, as psychiatrist W. Beran Wolfe put it, "The cultivation of mental elasticity is the best insurance against melancholia, depression, and a sense of futility."

Now record your end time and answer the following questions *before* computing your reading time and speed.

1. Greg Haber had a successful Army career after continuing his education.
   (T) True; (F) False

2. Learning involves the entire body, not just the entire brain.
   (T) True; (F) False

3. To get the most benefit from learning, it should be related to your job.
   (T) True; (F) False

4. When Emily and Ralph Peters replaced their calisthenics class with a course in archaeology, they still felt the need for more physical exercise.
   (T) True; (F) False

5. According to one quote from the Gerontology Center at the University of Southern California, "Continuing education over the life span is not only desirable; it may become essential."
   (T) True; (F) False

6. According to this article, continuing education promotes:
   a. mental well-being
   b. physical well-being
   c. ability to concentrate
   d. longevity
   e. all of these

7. In interviews with people in their sixties who have returned to the classroom, which is *not* a typical reaction?
   a. "It's the surest way to keep my mind active."
   b. "I want to train for a retirement career to keep myself active."
   c. "These courses have made a new woman/man out of me."
   d. "The classroom is the best medicine there is for an adult who wants to stay healthy and enjoy life."

8. People who pursue education on their own can get the same benefits as people who take structured curricula.
   (T) True (F) False

9. The author feels that the *best* educational programs are
   a. any that get the participants involved and motivated
   b. ones that balance mental and physical stamina
   c. ones that provide specific sequences of study, cultivate regular activity, and have forms of evaluation
   d. ones that promote lifelong learning habits

10. In conclusion, the author feels that
    a. the relationship between education and health has now been proven.
    b. evidence of learning's positive effects continues to mount.

c. cultivation of mental elasticity is the best insurance against depression.
d. "b" and "c."
e. "a," "b," and "c."

Now consult the table to get your reading speed. For example, if your reading time is 1 minute, 30 seconds, then your reading speed is 830 words per minute (wpm).

min.:sec.	1:30	1:40	1.50	2:00	2:10	2:20
wpm	830	750	680	625	575	535
min.:sec.	2:30	2:40	2:50	3:00	3:10	3:20
wpm	500	470	440	415	395	375
min.:sec.	3:30	3:40	3:50	4:00	4:10	4:20
wpm	355	340	325	310	300	290
min.:sec.	4:30	4:40	4:50	5:00	5:10	5:20
wpm	280	270	260	250	240	235
min.:sec.	5:30	5:40	5:50	6:00	6:20	6:40
wpm	225	220	215	210	200	190
min.:sec.	7:00	7:30	8:00			
wpm	180	170	155			

Record your speed on this page or on a separate sheet of paper.

Your speed is ____ wpm.
Your comprehension is ____ percent.

Answer key:

Question:	1	2	3	4	5	6	7	8	9	10
Answer:	F	T	F	F	T	e	b	T	d	d

If you got all ten correct, your comprehension was 100 percent. If you got nine correct, it was 90 percent; eight correct, 80 percent; etc. Compare the results with your pretest.

MEMORY RHYTHMS

ON YOUR OWN

MAKING A TAPE OF SHORT LEXICAL UNITS

As you were reading the suggestion that you make a tape, you may have been thinking, "I'll bet this isn't as easy as it sounds." Actually, it's much easier than traditional "brute force" methods. The only tricky part is synchronizing the time of speaking four seconds and pausing four seconds. One easy approach is to use a metronome. Set the metronome ticking in the background at one tick per second. Then when you are ready to record, speak your unit for four ticks and pause for four ticks.

If you don't have a metronome, the last ten minutes of side two of the *Learning Power* tape from Powerlearning® Systems has a recording of a metronome ticking. Then you can play this tape in the background while you make your supermemory tape. Every fourth beat has the crash of a tambourine. To setup the lexical units, it sounds like this. CRASH—click—click—click—CRASH—click—click—click.

Making your tape with this method requires two tape recorders. Use a small, inexpensive recorder in the background to play the metronome. Meanwhile, record your list into a better-quality recorder. Leave the first minute or two of the tape blank; then listen to the pattern of clicks until you are ready.

As the tambourine crashes, speak your first short lexical unit until it crashes again. Then pause. With the next crash, speak your next lexical unit until it crashes again. Then pause again, etc.

If you have only a few words in your lexical unit, speak a little more slowly. If you have eight or nine words, speak more quickly. If you end a little before or after the tambourine, it doesn't matter. The units should be *about* four seconds.

If you want to avoid the clicking on your tape, you can connect an earplug or headphones to the recorder with the metronome tape. Then you will hear the beat in your ear, speak perfect lexical units, and avoid rerecording the metronome. In fact, I strongly recommend that you use headphones. Otherwise the rerecorded clicking may distract you later.

MAKING A TAPE OF EXTENDED LEXICAL UNITS

If you are recording extended lexical units, the process is much simpler. Read the complete lexical unit into the recorder and then count inside your head, "one one hundred, two one hundred, three one hundred, four one hundred." Then speak the next unit, and count again. You may want to check your counting against a watch, but usually it's accurate enough. Of course, a disadvantage of the extended units is that you can't do the breathing pattern.

Remember, once you've recorded your tape, you have a choice. If the material is not too difficult to remember, making the tape is enough. If it is especially difficult, play it back, read along silently from the list, and do the breathing if appropriate. This completes setting up your memory rhythms.

MEMORY RHYTHMS WITH SHORT LEXICAL UNITS

Short lexical units (seven to nine words or less) can be spoken comfortably in four seconds. It's a great way to organize foreign words, short foreign phrases, short to moderate equations, technical terms, short to moderate spelling words, etc.

- List the units you want to memorize.
- Set a metronome, or play a recorded metronome on one tape recorder for your friend's timing or to record a tape.

On your own:
- If you are making a tape, use two tape recorders—one for the metronome and one for your voice. Leave the first one to two minutes blank, and then speak the first lexical unit. Remember to speak for about four ticks, pause for four ticks, speak for four ticks, pause for four ticks, etc.
- You can use an earplug or headphones with the metronome tape recorder to avoid rerecording the clicks.
- Record one or two minutes of faster baroque music at the end of the material. We will explain the use of music in later sections.
- If the material is not too difficult to remember, just making the tape is enough, and you are done with the active organizing.
- If the material is difficult to remember, play the tape back and *read silently from the list.*
- You can also use the breathing pattern. Hold in your breath while the voice is speaking. Then breathe out and in during the four-second pause.

With a friend:
- If you are studying with a friend, he or she reads one copy of the list aloud and uses the metronome for timing.
- You read along silently from your copy of the list and do the breathing pattern.

MEMORY RHYTHMS WITH EXTENDED LEXICAL UNITS

An extended lexical unit is a single point or principle expressed in one sentence. If the principle involves several sentences, each sentence is a single extended unit. Extended lexical units may include points from law, longer foreign phrases or spelling words, steps to solve an equation, etc.

• List the units you want to memorize.

On your own:
• If you are making a tape, leave the first one to two minutes blank. Then speak the complete lexical unit and pause for four seconds while silently counting, "one one hundred, two one hundred, three one hundred, four one hundred."
• Speak the next unit and again pause for four seconds, etc. Continue through your list.
• At the end of the tape, record one or two minutes of faster baroque music. Again, we will discuss the use of music later.
• If the material is not too difficult, just making the tape is enough. If the material is difficult to remember, play the tape back and read along silently from the list.
• With extended lexical units, do not use the breathing pattern.

With a friend:
• If you are working with a friend, that person reads from his or her copy of the script aloud while you read along silently from your copy of the list.

NOTES

CHAPTER ONE

1. Eric Jensen, *Student Success Secrets* (Woodbury, N.Y.: Barron's, 1989), pp. 17–19.

CHAPTER TWO

1. Tony Buzan, *Use Both Sides of Your Brain* (New York: E. P. Dutton, 1979). Buzan has coined the term *mind maps* for similar patterns. He has used them extensively as a tool for organizing notes, while Gabrielle Rico in *Writing the Natural Way* (Los Angeles: Jeremy P. Tarcher, 1983), has used a variation—"clustering" as a powerful tool to overcome "writer's block." Powerlearning uses this method as a way to display magic keys and other patterns of thought.
2. Steve and Connirae Andreas, *The Heart of the Mind* (Moab, UT.: Real People Press, 1989), pp. 155–165.

CHAPTER THREE

1. Peter Russell, *The Brain Book* (New York: Hawthorn Books, 1979), p. 36.
2. Tony Buzan, *Use Both Sides of Your Brain* (New York: E. P. Dutton, 1979), pp. 16–17.
3. Win Wenger, *How to Increase Your Intelligence* (New York: Dell Publishing, 1975), p. 35.
4. Jacquelyn Wonder and Priscilla Donovan, *Whole Brain Thinking* (New York: William Morrow, 1984), pp. 18–20.
5. Ibid., pp. 18–20.
6. Ibid., pp. 18–20.
7. Gabrielle Rico, *Writing the Natural Way* (Los Angeles: Jeremy P. Tarcher, 1983), p. 189.
8. David Lewis and James Green, *Thinking Better* (New York: Holt, Rinehart, & Winston, 1982), pp. 8–13. This book touches briefly on memory and learning but is primarily a pioneering work on critical and logical thinking skills. Three of my four fables (1, 2, and 4) are discussed here.
9. Robert True, "Experimental Control in Hypnotic Age Regression," *Science* 110:583–84.
10. Geoffrey Naylor and Else Hardwood, "Old Dogs, New Tricks: Age and Ability," *Psychology Today* (British), (April 1975), pp. 29–33.

CHAPTER FOUR

1. Some of the test questions are adapted and from several sources:

   • Jacquelyn Wonder and Priscilla Donovan, *Whole Brain Thinking* (New York: William Morrow, 1984), pp. 31–36.
   • Sharon Crain, *Self-Presentation for the Professional*, seminar and workbook (Palo Alto, Calif.: June 1985) pp. 1–16.
   • David Lewis and James Green, *Thinking Better* (New York: Holt, Rinehart, & Winston, 1982), pp. 149–50.

2. The labels "cerebral," "doer," "facilitator," and "expressive" have been used in other personality inventory tests. Wonder and Donovan, op. cit., were the first to interpret these in the framework of the right-brain/left-brain model.

CHAPTER FIVE

1. Sharon Crain, "Self-Presentation for the Professional" seminar and workbook (Palo Alto, Calif.: June 1985) and Jacquelyn Wonder and Priscilla Donovan, *Whole Brain Thinking* (New York: William Morrow, 1984). Dr. Crain discusses *fogging*, a well-known tool in the context of the right-brain/left-brain model. Wonder and Donovan discuss the problems of boredom and talking on the telephone, also based on the right-brain/left brain model. The love-letter technique has been successfully used for some years by the Catholic Church in their marriage encounter weekend. I have interpreted this technique and the problem of being stuck on a detailed problem in terms of the left and right sides of the brain.
2. Crain, op. cit.
3. Wonder and Donovan, op. cit. The authors present some of the techniques for right-and left-brain thinking in this and the next sections.
4. "Just How the Sexes Differ," *Newsweek* (May 18, 1981), and Jo Durden-Smith, "Male and Female—Why?" *Quest/80* (October 1980). These two articles discuss developmental differences in the sexes with age. These differences are interpreted here in terms of the left- and right-brain specializations and the thicker corpus collosum women generally have.
5. Tony Buzan, *Make the Most of Your Brain* (New York: Simon & Schuster, 1984), pp. 63–72. Buzan presents a nice discussion on hearing, listening, and memory. He touches on the concept of generalized vs. focused learning without calling it that.

CHAPTER SIX

----

1. Eric Jensen, *Student Success Secrets* (Woodbury, N.Y.: Barron's, 1989), p. 121.
2. This is quoted from Mark Van Doren in *Instant Memory* (Pacific Palisades, Calif: Institute of Advanced Thinking, 1972), p. 3.
3. *New Scientist* (October 9, 1980). Researchers at the University of Cambridge tested subjects at 10:00 A.M., 3:00 P.M., and at 7:00 P.M. on long-term memory. The subjects at 7:00 P.M. scored highest and the ones at 10:00 A.M. scored lowest.
4. These categories are adapted and modified from Peter Russell, *The Brain Book* (New York: Hawthorn Books, 1979), p. 237.
5. George Miller, "The Magic Number Seven, Plus or Minus Two: Some Limits in Our Capacity for Processing Information," *Psychological Review*, Vol. 63, pp. 81–97.
6. Hermann Ebbinghaus, *Memory*, trans. D. H. Ruyer and C. E. Bussenius (New York: Teachers College Press, 1913).
7. *American Journal of Psychiatry* (February 1978). Researchers from UCLA divided a group of smokers into two groups. Each member of the control group smoked a nonnicotine cigarette, while each in the experimental group smoked a regular one. On a memory test afterward, the experimental group scored 24 percent lower.
8. *Journal of Studies of Alcohol* (January 1980). Researchers at the University of Oklahoma Health Sciences Center studied young to middle-aged women before and after drinking. Memory was not only impaired by the immediate drink, but also the more years the subjects had been drinking, the greater the effect on memory. Some memory loss even carried into times the subjects were not drinking.
9. *Newsweek* (September 29, 1986), pp. 48–54.
10. Ibid.
11. *The Sybervision Foreign Language Series—Instruction Manual* (Pleasanton, Calif., Sybervision, 1988), pp. 2–14.
12. *Prevention* (February 1985), p. 123.
13. Colin Rose, *Accelerated Learning* (New York: Dell, 1985), p. 16.
14. George Korona, Organizing and Memorizing (New York: Columbia University Press, 1972).

CHAPTER SEVEN
----

1. P. McKellar, "The Investigation of Mental Images, *Penguin Science Survey* (London: Penguin, 1965).
2. Ralph N. Haber, "How We Remember What We See," *Scientific American* (May 1970), p. 105.
3. Gordon Bower, "Mental Imagery and Associative Learning," *Cognition in Learning and Memory* (New York: John Wiley, 1972), p. 69.
4. Several suggestions are adapted from Tony Buzan, *Make the Most of Your Brain* (New York: Simon & Schuster, 1984), pp. 63–72.
5. Jacquelyn Wonder and Priscilla Donovan, *Whole Brain Thinking* (New York: William Morrow, 1984), and SALT teacher training course (Summer 1982), Iowa State University, Ames, Ia. Wonder and Donovan cite research from the Center for the Advancement of Creative Persons and University Associates and from the Synectic Institute of Massachusetts as supporting these statistics.
6. Duncan R. Godden and Alan D. Baddeley, "Context Dependent Memory in Two Natural Environments: On Land and Under Water," *British Journal of Psychology*, Vol. 66, pp. 325–32.

CHAPTER EIGHT
----

1. Sheila Ostrander and Lynn Schroeder, *Superlearning*® (New York: Dell Publishing, 1979), p. 19.
2. S. Krashen and T. Terrell, *The Natural Approach to Language Acquisition* (Oxford: Pergamon Press, 1983).
3. Ibid., Chaps. 2 and 3.
4. Ostrander and Schroeder, op. cit., and D. H. Schuster and C. E. Gritton, *Suggestive Accelerative Learning Techniques* (New York: Gordon and Breach Science Publishers, 1986). The latter describes this step as an "active organizing" phase for teachers, while *Superlearning*® describes an organizing step for students to use the method on their own.
5. Colin Rose, *Accelerated Learning* (New York: Dell, 1985), p. 93.
6. Ostrander and Schroeder, op. cit., p. 125.

7. Rose, *op. cit.*, p. 102.
8. Ostrander and Schroeder, *op. cit.*, p. 51.
9. Lin Doherty at "Mastery of Magic," a presentation on NLP and accelerated learning methods for teachers, (June–July 1985), Santa Barbara, Calif.

CHAPTER NINE
----

1. Tony Buzan, *Use Both Sides of Your Brain* (New York: E. P. Dutton, 1979), pp. 35–47.
2. Eric Jensen, *Student Success Secrets* (New York: Barron's, 1989), p. 81, and Buzan, ibid., p. 31.

CHAPTER TEN
----

1. B. Zeigarnik, "Das Behalten erledigter und unerleddigter Handungen," *Psychologisch Forschung* 9:1–85.
2. P. Russell, *The Brain Book* (New York: Hawthorn Books, 1979) and Tony Buzan, *Use Both Sides of Your Brain* (New York: E. P. Dutton, 1979). Buzan and Russell each suggest this "modular learning" approach, with a break every thirty to forty minutes, based on Zeigarik's findings. Each presents the graph I have shown of how the memory curve is modified with these changes.
4. Russell, op. cit., and C. Rose, *Accelerated Learning* (New York: Dell, 1985). Russell and Rose each recommended the four to five reviews with the timing as I've suggested in this section. This pattern is consistent with research on how to improve the normal Ebbinghaus curve, and this timing facilitates transfer from short-term to long-term memory.
5. John Ott, *Health and Light* (Old Greenwich, Conn.: Devin-Adair, 1973).
6. Adapted from Buzan, op. cit., pp. 137–147. Buzan's approach is similar to SALT in establishing a broad right-brain perspective first and then focusing on finer left-brain detail.
7. With each eye the left half of the field of vision goes to the right

side of the brain, while the right half of each field of vision goes to the left side of the brain.

CHAPTER ELEVEN

----

1. P. Airola, *Are You Confused?* (Phoenix: Health Plus Publishers, 1971), Chap. 2 and p. 54.
2. Ibid., pp. 52–53.

CHAPTER TWELVE

----

1. *New Age Journal* (November 1977), p. 24. This article reports on a study of the mental and emotional benefits of exercise with school-age children.
2. "Why Children Should Draw," *Saturday Review* (September 3, 1977), pp. 11–16.
3. Win Wenger, *An Easy Way to Increase Your Intelligence* (Gaithersburg, Md.: Psychogenics Press).
4. "The Edith Project", *The Sunday Times* (London) (April 17, 1977).
5. C. Rose, *Accelerated Learning* (New York: Dell, 1985), p. 21.
6. J. Altman, "Autoradiographic and Histological Studies of Postnatal Neurogenesis: II. A Longitudinal Investigation of the Kinetics and Transformation of Cells Incorporating Tritiated Thymidine in Infant Rats, with Special Reference to Postnatal Neurogenesis in Some Brain Regions," *Journal of Comparative Neurology* CXXVIII, (1966); Gopal D. Das, "Autoradiographic Examination of the Effects of Enriched Environment on the Rate of Glial Multiplication in the Adult Rat Brain," *Nature* CCIV (December 19, 1964).
7. J. P. Banquet, "Spectral Analysis of EEG in Meditation," *Electroencephalography and Clinical Neurophysiology* (1975), p. 35.
8. Allan I. Abrams, "Paired–Associate Learning and Recall: A Pilot Study of the Transcendental Meditation Technique" (Berkeley: University of California), *Scientific Research on the Transcendental Meditation Program: Collected Papers* (New York: MIU Press, 1975).
9. Arthur Aaron, David Orme-Johnson, and Paul Brubaker, "The Transcendental Meditation Program in the College Curriculum: A

Four-Year Longitudinal Study of Effects on Cognitive and Affective Functioning," *College Student Journal* 15 (1981), pp. 140–46.

10. R. K. Wallace, M. Dillbeck, E. Jacobe, and B. Harrington, "The Effects of the Transcendental Meditation and TM Sidhis Program on the Aging Process," *International Journal of Neuroscience* 16 (1982), pp. 53–58.

11. D. H. Schuster and C. E. Gritton, *Suggestive Accelerative Learning Techniques* (New York: Gordon and Breach Science Publishers, 1986).

APPENDIX ONE

1. Thor Heyerdahl, "From Plankton to Whales," *The Kon-Tiki Expeditions* (George Allen & Unwin: 1950) reprinted in Horace Judson, *The Techniques of Reading* (New York: Harcourt Brace Jovanovich, 1972), pp. 30–32.

2. Judson, *op. cit.*, pp. 32–33.

3. *Ibid.* p. 475.

APPENDIX TWO

1. Horace Judson, *The Techniques of Reading* (New York: Harcourt Brace Jovanovich, 1972), pp. 54–56.

2. *Ibid.*, pp. 476–479.

APPENDIX THREE

1. William Cross, "Surprising Rx for a Richer, Happier Life," *Reader's Digest*, vol. 120, April, 1982, pp. 138–140.

POWERLEARNING ®

SYSTEMS

We all want to live our lives to the fullest. Everyone wants to learn new things . . . a foreign language, a new hobby, computers, university course work, or how to advance our careers; yet many of us feel blocked. We have in the human brain the gift of nature's most superb engineering feat, but we were not given an instruction manual.

Powerlearning® Systems offers seminars, consultation, books, and tapes that provide the most advanced technologies available today to accelerate learning and have fun in the process.

For information on available services and products write to

Dr. Don Lofland
Powerlearning® Systems
P.O. Box 496
Santa Cruz, CA 95060

- Corporate Seminars
- In Service Trainings for Teachers
- Individual Consultations
- Accelerated Learning Books, Tapes, & Resources
- Foreign Language Courses.